WITHDRAWN
UTSA LIBRARIES

Robert Delavignette on the French Empire

Studies in Imperialism
Robert W. Winks, Editor

Edited by William B. Cohen
*with the assistance
of Adelle Rosenzweig*

Robert Delavignette on the French Empire
Selected Writings

Selections Translated by
Camille Garnier

The University of Chicago Press
Chicago and London

The University of Chicago Press, Chicago 60637
The University of Chicago Press, Ltd., London

©1977 by The University of Chicago
All rights reserved. Published 1977

Printed in the United States of America
81 80 79 78 77   987654321

WILLIAM B. COHEN is associate professor of
history at Indiana University. He is the author
of *Rulers of Empire: The French Colonial
Service in Africa.*

Library of Congress Cataloging in Publication Data

Delavignette, Robert Louis, 1897–1976
    Robert Delavignette on the French Empire.

    (Studies in imperialism)
    Bibliography: p.
    Includes index.
    1. France—Colonies—History. 2. France—Colo-
nies—Administration.   I. Cohen, William B.,
1941–   II. Rosenzweig, Adelle.   III. Title.
JV1818.D4   325′.344   77–1339
ISBN 0–226–14191–8

Contents

Series Editor's Preface

One of the greatest needs in the study of imperialism is for a series of careful monographic biographies of those who either called themselves, or are labeled by others, "imperialists." The literature in the field is rich in administrative and legal histories, in books on military events, and in theoretical statements. The last, in particular, tend so to concentrate on the broad sweep of events, or on the interaction between impersonal economic factors and specific colonial situations, as almost to ignore the individual. This tendency to ignore individual motivation in history has always been common to economic history, of course, and the study of imperialism often has been thought to be a branch of economic scholarship. The unsatisfactory result is that we do not know in any detail precisely what figure X did that may intersect with theory Y.

The problem is at least as serious with autobiography, for imperial authors seem seldom to have been introspective enough to fulfill the demands of a genuinely revealing self-study: their autobiographies are written as though at one time (as many were), without any evidence that the act of writing the autobiography itself forced upon the author a reevaluation of the deeds being described. As Roy Pascal has noted in *Design and Truth in Autobiography*, no self-study can be considered to be true unless the author catches himself by surprise, as it were, in the writing and reveals that surprise as part of his growth to the reader. By this criterion, few autobiographies are successful, and given the overlay of ideology and the need for justification that is the usual freight of most imperialists' accounts of their work, imperial history shows few instances of this kind of self-awareness and discovery.

Robert Delavignette seems more than most to have been able to see himself plain. As William B. Cohen points out in the introduction to this selection from the French administrator's writings, Delavignette expressed his sense of irony in a pseudonymous novel, *Toum*. But his signed writings also show the healthy ambivalence so necessary to writing about empire, as well as the touch of the icicle at the heart essential to the historian. The present volume, therefore, is unusual in its contribution to an understanding of imperialism in general, and it provides us with many windows into the specifically French nature of the imperial experience.

ROBIN W. WINKS

Preface

The purpose of this work is to acquaint the reader with the inner workings of the French colonial system through an examination of the writings of a significant French overseas official, Robert Delavignette. While unique in its vision and prescience, much of Delavignette's thinking reflects that which was best within the French colonial tradition. Since he was connected with many of the major experiences of the French empire, his thought and writings should help explain the nature of French colonialism.

Delavignette was an optimist and an idealist who revealed to his superiors and to the French public the gap which existed between French ideals and accomplishments. At times he believed that the goals which he wished to see accomplished had come closer to being realized than was actually the case, and thus there is in his writings a certain idealization of the French empire. Such passages, which will be obvious to the reader, reflect an important strain within French imperial strivings. At other times Delavignette was a bitter critic who decried the betrayal by France of her overseas mission; these passages reveal the extent to which even contemporaries within the French colonial bureaucracy could detect the shortcomings of French colonialism.

Because he served at all levels of the colonial bureaucracy for nearly forty years Delavignette's writings reflect the problems which faced the local bush administrator as well as those which were of concern to the highest policy-makers in Paris. These writings span the era from the zenith of French colonial strength immediately after World War I to the trauma of decolonization and then the readjustment in relationships that occurred in the 1960s between France and her former overseas territories.

Each chapter has an introduction stating the nature of the selections that follow. The numbers in parentheses in the introductions are the numbers of the selections that follow and also of the sources for the selections that are listed at the end of each chapter. To make the selections more readable, I have omitted the punctuation which is traditionally used to indicate an ellipsis.

Two important works, *Service africain* and *Christianisme et colonialisme*, are not represented in this work since they have been translated into English and are thus readily available.* Readers of these works will, however, recognize similar ideas and experiences in this collection.

*Translated as *Freedom and Authority in French West Africa* (London, 1950), *Christianity and Colonialism* (New York, 1964).

Introduction
The Career of
Robert Delavignette

The career and writings of Robert Delavignette span more than a half-century of French colonialism, from its apogee in the 1920s to its demise in 1960. Delavignette served as clerk; district administrator; the chief administrative assistant to the reform-minded Popular Front minister of colonies in 1936; director of the Ecole nationale de la France d'outre-mer (ENFOM), the institution that trained overseas administrators; commissioner of the Cameroons, in 1946–47; the highest permanent official of the ministry of colonies; and finally, in 1951, in a return to the colonial school, an instructor there. After his retirement from public office in 1957 he continued to be closely concerned with the problems of the former empire. That Delavignette occupied many of his posts of responsibility for relatively short periods of time reveals the French colonial tradition of rapid personnel turnover and the lack of appreciation for the value of a stable administration. But the short periods of service are also a tribute to Delavignette, in that they reflect the extent to which various branches of the overseas administration often felt it necessary to call upon him, at critical junctures.

Delavignette's writings are a valuable source of information on French colonialism because they are the product of a man with a varied and long colonial experience. His ideas are important because they had a wide audience and were highly respected by contemporary readers. If any one person were to be chosen as a shaper of public opinion on colonial matters after World War I, that person would be Robert Delavignette. His ideas are representative of the "humanitarian colonial"[1] school which developed in France in the 1930s. These ideas gained a particular following among young people and motivated a number of them to enter the colonial service.

1

Through countless books and hundreds of newspaper and magazine articles, Delavignette attempted to educate an essentially indifferent public about colonial problems. He stressed in his writings the culture and personality of the colonial peoples: they were not quaint objects for travel films; they were men and women with a history and a culture; they had their own dreams and ambitions. By establishing control over these peoples, the French state had acquired certain obligations toward them. There were serious responsibilities which fell upon Frenchmen, there were economic sacrifices that would have to be made for the impoverished peasants of the Sudanic belt and the Tonkin delta. Comfortable modes of thought conveniently stereotyping the colonial peoples as primitive and barbarian needed to be discarded to allow a totally new relationship to emerge between the motherland and the overseas possessions. While Delavignette was vague, presumably these changes would be reflected in some institutional manner within the imperial structure, giving the colonies greater power to determine their fate.

To young African intellectuals in Paris, Delavignette represented that which was best in the French tradition. Africans were drawn to him and found him a sympathetic listener. He knew and admired African peasant society but also had an appreciation for the young, black intellectuals in Paris trying to assert the genius of their culture, to express what came to be known as *négritude*. Delavignette helped the literary careers of a number of young blacks by reviewing or even writing prefaces for their works, thus making them known to the public. After World War II Delavignette continued to express great sympathy for the values of negritude and to nourish close personal relations with some of the most influential members of the main organ of negritude, *Présence africaine*. Thus Delavignette's writings and career symbolize a kind of bridge between two communities, the French and the African. While in Africa he had been the white man's representative; in Paris he was the interpreter of the black man's culture. As President Léopold Senghor of Senegal has written, "What makes Robert Delavignette a pioneer ... is that in the colonial era itself he overcame the dichotomy white-black, Europe-Africa, in order to create a symbiosis."[2] Thus he proudly remained a man of two cultures, believing that each culture could be enriched and fulfilled by being true to its own values at the same time as it assimilated values from the other.

Robert Delavignette was born in Sainte Colombe sur Seine in 1897 in the old province of Burgundy. His family was of moderate means, the father working in a managerial capacity at a small iron-smelting works. The picture which emerges from Delavignette's writings about his youth is one of a relatively happy time. It certainly was not socially restricted; he spent much of his free time in the forge talking to the workers and absorbing their tales about life in the old days and the various legends associated with the career of the smith. He had his secondary education in Dijon, going to the lycée there. His teachers were evidently remarkable individuals, and he seems to have been especially affected by two: Professor Auguste Mairey, a geographer, and Professor Gaston Roupnel, an historian. Mairey opened to the young Delavignette the large vistas of the world, and it might be surmised that overseas France was also stressed in these geography lessons. (In a geography textbook that Mairey had published, more space was spent on the empire than was common at that time.)[3] Roupnel was part of the distinguished tradition of French social historians which was to find its culmination in men like Marc Bloch. Like Bloch, Roupnel stressed the importance of the social foundations of French history: it was not the kings of France who had made the country but the tillers of the soil, generations of whom, by their efforts and suffering, had made human progress possible. The peasant was central to Roupnel's history. It was through Roupnel's influence that Delavignette developed an empathy for the common people and determined to understand their culture and life-style.

These are Delavignette's own memories of his development, and for the teacher who wishes to believe in the efficacy of his efforts these explanations are of course very encouraging. But one can ask why Delavignette was so receptive to his teachers. Had he not already in his father's forge revealed great empathy for the common man? And before coming under Mairey's influence had he not voraciously been devouring the descriptions of exotic lands in the pages of the then popular journals *Illustration* and *Tours du monde*? These interests seem to have been awakened before he arrived at the lycée in Dijon, but there of course they had a chance to develop further.

Delavignette graduated from the lycée in 1914. In 1916 he was drafted, sent to the Front, and wounded. Like so many sensitive men of his generation, young Delavignette seems to have had some glimpse of the mixture of heroism, folly, and cowardice that animated what was known as the Great War. What he found most despicable was the callous manner in which officers ordered men to their death merely to gain an advance of a few yards and thus win honors or promotion. Sixty years later anger still entered his voice as he recalled the soldiers who died solely to satisfy the *amour propre* of some officer. This war experience made Delavignette suspicious of the official mind, which so often is blind to the needs of real people.

In 1919, along with the rest of the French army, Delavignette was demobilized. He now had to decide on a career. It was expected that he would follow in his father's footsteps and work in the forge, but the destruction which had been wrought both physically and spiritually upon Europe made leaving for what seemed like the unlimited horizons of the colonial world more attractive to him. Delavignette applied for and was appointed as colonial clerk to French West Africa. He was assigned to Dakar in the central bureaucracy of the French West African federation. He seems to have been annoyed by the petty tasks of his work, and a year later, when the opportunity arose, he entered the Colonial School in Paris. The training was to qualify him as a colonial administrator.

Upon graduating from the Colonial School, Delavignette was assigned in 1922 as administrator third class to serve in the finance bureau in Niger. Zinder, an ancient caravan town where nomads from the desert traded with the sedentary people, was still a rather picturesque city that reminded the young Frenchman of the world of the *Arabian Nights* or of the Old Testament. Sitting in the treasury office, Delavignette yearned for the day when he would administer his own district and perhaps emulate Commandant Fleury, the administrator of Zinder, who, with red beard flowing, rode in hot pursuit of horse thieves and was appropriately nicknamed "horse-thief catcher." Delavignette had to wait only a few months for his assignment. In February 1923 he was appointed administrator of the subdivision of Tessao, located west of Zinder. And a few months later he was again reassigned, this time to Dosso. This kind of instability in the administration was common, but at least Delavignette was fortunate enough to remain in the same general region. These were Islamized regions with large nomadic populations whose relationships with the sedentary peoples were always difficult; the age-old struggle between nomad and peasant went on unabated here. The former tended to dominate, and the young administrator interfered when he thought their rule became overly harsh and arbitrary.[4]

Although Delavignette saw French rule as a beneficent force, he by no means shared in the generally low respect for the local chiefs that French administrators usually exhibited. The sultans of the upper Sudan often had sophisticated governments which had a firm control over their subjects. To ignore the traditional ruler was usually a sure way to invite chaos and anarchy. An administrator could not afford to take such risks. So Delavignette's early experience with traditional rule convinced him that the French administration must prevent the worst abuses of cruelty and dishonesty among the chiefs but still respect the general institution of traditional rulership and attempt to work through it. A similar approach had been developed and its rationale fully articulated in neighboring Nigeria, where the British had to deal with even more powerful emirates which could not readily be crushed. Delavignette's ideas were probably an amalgam of his experience in the field and the example of the neighboring British in Nigeria. While many French administrators were uninterested in the British or for that matter in the experiences of other European nations in the colonies, Delavignette seems to have been well aware of both.

In addition to developing some notions about "native policy," Delavignette came to know intimately the difficulty of being given orders by his superiors but not having the means to effect them. In Niger he also experienced loneliness in the midst of people—a people who did not share his culture and language. Living side by side, the European and the African had many reasons to misunderstand each other. The ironies inherent in such a situation were fully explored by Delavignette in a little novel he published in 1926 called *Toum*. Because it did not always present colonial rule favorably, it was written under the pseudonym of "Louis Faivre."[5] He continued to write colonial articles under that pseudonym.

After serving in the Sahel region, Delavignette was transferred to the south, to Upper Volta. In Ougadougou he served as assistant to the district officer, the *commandant de cercle*, from November 1925 to January 1927. While he had not particularly liked the red tape and dreariness of desk administration, he seems to have done well, and his superior, the *commandant de cercle* of Ougadougou, wrote in 1926, "This is a first-class official who will always be the right man, be it in the bush or in an office."[6] After a leave, he was assigned to Banfora, in the bush in Upper Volta. The administrative subdivision of Banfora was one of three in the *cercle* of Bobo Diallasso. The *commandant de cercle* located in Bobo was responsible for the whole *cercle* but direct responsibility rested with the *chef de subdivision* of Banfora, Delavignette. The region had a population of approximately 100,000.[7] Each village had its chief, and these in turn were responsible to an African appointed by the French, the *chef de canton*. There were nine of these in the subdivision of Banfora. Immediately above them was the *chef de subdivision*. As head of the subdivision, Delavignette had all the responsibilities of a *commandant de cercle*, with the exception that he was formally responsible to the *commandant* in Bobo Diallasso.

The region of Banfora had been a turbulent one which the French had had considerable trouble controlling. In 1915 it had been the scene of a violent uprising that had been put down only with the greatest difficulty. Using the common device of "divide and rule" the French had brought in the Ouattara, a people from the Kong region of the Ivory Coast to help suppress the inhabitants. In reward for their efforts the Ouattara were made chiefs of the region. They were hated by the local inhabitants, and they in turn had utter contempt for the people over whom they had been given rulership. Forgetting that the French had put them in a position of authority, they felt they had a right to rule unfettered by European intervention. When in late 1927 the French administrator of Banfora, Livmann, fired the *chef de canton* in that district, the Ouattara precipitated violence and on January 3, 1928, Livmann was stabbed and had to be medically evacuated.[8]

It was under these difficult circumstances that Delavignette was appointed head of the Banfora subdivision. He had had sufficient experience with ethnic strife of various sorts, especially in Niger. By skillful diplomacy, a series of palavers with village elders, he was able to get the would-be assassin delivered up and to reestablish tranquility in the region.

Banfora was a poor region with few economic resources; the peasants lived at the subsistence level and sometimes below it. Delavignette saw his role as ensuring the economic welfare of the people in his district as well as restoring peace in the region.

In the 1920s the colonial administration established seed cooperatives in West Africa; under government auspices millet and other foods were stored for the following year to ensure that there would be sufficient seed to plant for the new harvest. Delavignette actively encouraged the local peasantry to contribute to the cooperative. The world demand for peanuts was high, and Delavignette saw it as a cash crop which would give the people of his district much-needed money. He toured his district preaching the cultivation of peanuts. The peasants were naturally suspicious but overcame their reluctance and followed the French administrator's advice. In 1927 450 tons were grown in the district. Production increased nearly tenfold during the following two years: in 1928 and 1929 8,000 tons were gathered. The peanuts, also known as groundnuts, were exploited for their oil. They had to be pressed by hand, an inefficient method which yielded only half the oil that could be obtained by using an industrial press. When Delavignette helped bring an industrial press to Banfora,[9] it freed much of the population from the backbreaking work of extracting the oil, and the laborers could concentrate instead on food crops or on more peanut production. The success of the groundnut harvests of 1928 and 1929 created a sense of well-being in the population. Delavignette's espousal of cash crop production was very much a part of the concern of the interwar French administration. Not only did his district produce large amounts of crops, but Delavignette himself, unlike many of his colleagues, was interested in seeing that the newly created wealth went to the people who had labored for it. In many districts the chiefs forcibly extracted labor from their subjects while withholding from them the fruits of their efforts. French administrators often condoned such behavior, being interested only in the high production attained in their districts. But Delavignette was genuinely concerned and, more by palaver than by force, seems to have convinced the chiefs and elders of the wisdom of letting all share in the newly created wealth. His method of administration was seen as a model, and Governor General Jules Brevié summarized his colonial career as follows:

> During his colonial assignments Delavignette has always obtained the best results at the head of the districts he has administered. Intelligent, energetic, having very good judgment and tact and very taken with his profession, he has acquired a profound knowledge of African affairs. A talented writer.[10]

As Brevié noted, Delavignette had become famous as a writer. His *Toum* and various journal articles on colonial affairs had gone unnoticed, but then in 1931, this time under his own name, the book appeared that created his fame, *Paysans noirs*. It was the account of a young administrator charged with a difficult district, having taken it over after the assassination of the previous administrator. The book was arranged in twelve chapters, one for each month. It detailed the progress of a colonial administrator and his district through the seasons of the year, from planting through harvest time.

The title of the book was significant. Frenchmen had become accustomed to thinking of the colonial peoples as faceless "natives." Delavignette restored to them a human significance. They were peasants, black peasants. It was his knowledge of French peasantry that helped him understand that Africans were not uniform, that they had local traditions and beliefs which deserved respect. Still, he did not deny Africans their own personality or make them merely some vague facsimile of the French peasantry. Like the French peasants, most Africans lived off the land; they were bound to it and their future depended upon how the soil was treated. The role of the French administration was to help develop that soil.

The administrator depicted in *Paysans noirs* respected the traditions of the elders and consulted at great length with them. By appeals to this tradition he sought support for the changes that were important if the community was to live at peace and in prosperity. Delavignette understood what few economic developers then—or for that matter since—have understood, and that is that development cannot be imposed from the outside. Change can come only when the people in a region are convinced of its advantages. Economic change must not be seen as a threat to a community's whole way of life but rather as a means of ensuring its survival. Delavignette described the changes as simultaneously saving the village life while auguring a new era. Thus the oil press in Banfora kept the young men from migrating southward by providing jobs. The community remained intact; the villages did not lose their young men. On the other hand the new income which the young men received allowed them to establish their own households and become more independent of their elders than had been the custom. Thus a new, freer social organization was evolving. Humane administration would permit the traditional societies to preserve much of their structure, but it was also creating a new Africa. Within African society there were forces susceptible of development, and it was these forces, according to Delavignette, that the French presence should encourage and guide.

The role of the administrator was to deal with people not in the abstract but very personally, at the village level and down to the household. The whole community's problems had become the administrator's concerns. In that sense, as Delavignette later was to write, the colonial administration was a totalitarian system.[11]

Unlike so much of the colonial literature that was self-sure of the white man's mission overseas, *Paysans noirs* was somewhat hesitant. The people in the story, black and white, were real human beings. The white administrator was at times filled with self-doubt: had he misled his subjects, would in fact the rains come? Would the elders, so much wiser and experienced, listen to a man in his twenties whom they still considered a boy? What if all the efforts came to naught? The attraction of the novel was that it was a profoundly realistic work depicting in rich detail the life of Africans and of French administrators overseas. It was immediately a success and won a prize as the best novel with a colonial theme in 1931. It was made into a movie and in 1946 reprinted in a new edition.

Delavignette's health had not been good while he was in Africa. He had acquired chronic malaria, some of his war wounds had acted up, and he suffered from a punctured ear drum. When the Agence économique pour l'Afrique occidentale française, located in Paris, offered him a post in 1931 he welcomed the chance to stay in France to regain his health. The position must have further tempted him since it allowed him to remain with his new bride, Annie Mairey (the widow of his geography teacher, who had been killed in World War I).

The role of the Agence was to attract investments and to spread information about Africa. Delavignette was ideally suited for the latter role. The opening of the international colonial exhibition of 1931 was accompanied by the publication of an ambitious series of volumes on the empire. Delavignette was commissioned to write the volume on French West Africa, *Afrique occidentale française*. Beautifully illustrated with wood engravings, the book was written in the style that had become his trademark. It was highly personal, revealing the experiences and feelings of the author while also including all the official statistics that are usually expected of such volumes.

In a series of journal articles Delavignette wrote about the Depression and its effect on Africa. He deplored the utopian notions of some publicists (usually political right-wingers) who were suggesting that French recovery could come from organized exploitation of the colonies. On the contrary, Delavignette insisted, it was a time to invest in the colonies and help them, for they too were hit by the worldwide economic crisis. The French government and people should be concerned not only with the poverty of Europe but also the misery of the African peasant. His needs were in many ways more pressing; often lacking the simplest amenities, such as a water well or iron plow, Africans were particularly subject to the vagaries of the weather and other uncontrollable forces. Delavignette was the advocate of "small projects"—the digging of wells or the installation of water pumps—that would have immediate impact on the daily life of a village. Grandiose plans for dams, railroad networks, and ports were important too, but they must not prevent the development of programs administering directly to human needs. In article after article Delavignette tried to educate the public in the needs of the colonies. If an empire united in purpose was to be created, it had to share the experience of self-sacrifice. Delavignette scored programs aimed at developing the colonies only the more readily to exploit them; what was needed was that people in the colonies experience a real improvement in their lot.

In 1934, on the occasion of the fiftieth anniversary of the French conquest of the Sudan, Delavignette made an official journey to the Sudan and subsequently published his *Soudan-Paris-Bourgogne*. The thesis of this book was that the Sudan was as much a province of France as Delavignette's own beloved Burgundy and, like it, had a right to its own life and personality. There was a symbiosis between these two provinces, Sudan and Burgundy, and Paris. They gave human meaning to the city; they both represented the historic verities of man, his age-old relationship with the soil and the traditions of his ancestors. Paris was pointing to the future, but in order to gain wisdom and balance it needed to draw on the life of its provinces. As he had already shown in *Paysans noirs*, Delavignette was able to combine a deep appreciation of tradition with commitment to change. Men's lives could be improved by technology. The oil press in Banfora had helped enrich the peasants; the dam being built on the Niger would help irrigate new fields for the Sudanese peasant. But for his life to have meaning, the individual, and the society of which he was a part, had to have a culture, a central focus of beliefs. Delavignette was not favoring the substitution of French culture for the African one. There were aspects of French culture, for instance its technological prowess, which would be useful to Africans. But the culture exchange was not to go only in one direction. Frenchmen had much to learn from their compatriots overseas, from their reverence for nature and the ability to live in harmony with it, and from their affirmation of spiritual values. By living together in a union in which each party would be allowed to preserve its own personality, the two peoples, by the interchange of values, would enrich the cultures of both. If Delavignette never quite spelled out what the future political configuration of the French empire might be, the general themes of his writings suggested a loose federation. His thoughts were parallel with those of his fellow administrator Henri Labouret, a former administrator of the Ivory Coast and a renowned ethnologist.

After World War I Frenchmen were optimistic about their empire. They saw in its allegiance to the mother country during the war evidence of the success of French colonialism. Colonial commentators were generally satisfied with the nature of the empire and its institutions; the celebrations surrounding the 1931 colonial exposition were a kind of apotheosis of French imperialism. Delavignette's writings were unusual in their critical posture amid the prevailing optimism. Beginning in the 1930s, he went against the grain of much of the common thinking on colonial questions, often anticipating the future evolution of the empire by as much as a decade. This constituted considerable prescience in a time of change such as the 1930s.

As a result of having fought in World War I, a large number of colonial troops returned home with a new sense of assertiveness; they no longer felt comfortable under the authoritarian rule which existed overseas. And in some cases they challenged it. Western education in the colonial schools spread the ideals both of democracy and nationalism, and these too undermined French authority. Young African intellectuals began to study in Paris, and there they came into contact with ideologies asserting the separate destiny of black peoples, the early formulations of the ideology that was to become negritude. Colonial authority overseas was to a large degree based on the force which the mother country had or pretended to have; the depression in France, the polarization of domestic politics, and the failure of France to play a role as a great power in European diplomacy in the 1930s potentially undermined all that. Delavignette understood that the claims of conquest half a century earlier no longer constituted sufficient basis for maintaining the empire and was one of the few men writing on colonial questions who argued for the establishment of a new relationship with the overseas territories.

Having won a certain reputation for his advocacy of overseas reform, Delavignette quite naturally was asked to collaborate in the Ministry of Colonies under the Popular Front government, which came to power in June 1936 supported by France's three largest political parties of the Left—the Socialist, Radical and Communist parties. The new minister of colonies, Marius Moutet, a Socialist, had a reputation as a critic of colonial abuse and was committed to bringing reforms overseas. He chose Delavignette as one of his main aides to handle the daily tasks of administration in the ministry. Delavignette had the confidence of his fellow administrators but was also sympathetic to the overall goals of the new minister. This usefulness was attested to by Moutet, who later was to say, "Delavignette was one of my best advisors. Whatever function he fulfilled he always was in control of the situation."[12]

Less than a year after his appointment to the Ministry of Colonies, Delavignette received a new assignment, as director of ENFOM, which trained French overseas administrators.

The school had been founded in 1887. For over a generation it had been a rather undistinguished institution that trained only a small proportion of the men in the colonial service. After World War I the Ministry of Colonies required that all men entering the Corps of Colonial Administrators have some training at the school. In 1926 it acquired a new director, Georges Hardy, who freed the future administrators from much of the traditional legal curriculum of the school and instead stressed courses which would more closely reflect the realities of overseas life through an increased emphasis on languages and ethnology.

Two directors served for short and undistinguished terms after Hardy, and in 1937 Delavignette was appointed. He built on Hardy's accomplishments, pushing further the emphasis on a curriculum reflecting the evolution overseas. He hired distinguished ethnologists such as Marcel Griaule and Jacques Soustelle. African language teachers were also brought to the school: Diori Hamani, who taught Hausa, and later Léopold Sédar Senghor, to teach Manding languages. Both these men were gifted individuals who in 1960 became presidents of their newly independent countries.

Delavignette introduced in the middle of the students' stay at the school a one-year training program in the colonies to give the future administrators practical experience, a concrete sense of the nature of colonial life. This program, however, was hardly in effect before World War II broke out and made the program impracticable. During the entire war the school stayed open and Delavignette remained its director. A large number of graduates continued to flow from the school. The colonial service offered an opportunity for young Frenchmen to flee their defeated, occupied homeland, and many seem to have believed that the glory that had been lost on the battlefields could be regained by glorious action in the colonies.

The curriculum of the school created a young group of administrators better in touch with colonial realities than had previously been the case. But Delavignette himself also helps explain the excitement and sense of commitment that animated the young graduates of ENFOM. He had very close contacts with his students, frequently having them to his home and introducing them to his African friends. His large frame led his students affectionately to nickname him "le grand Bob." Several former students named their sons after him and long after they had left ENFOM they continued to correspond with their former teacher. These contacts undoubtedly help explain why even after Delavignette had ceased going overseas he was so well informed on the evolution of the empire. Dozens of his correspondents throughout the empire, former students, continuously apprised him of what was going on at their levels of the administration, giving him information that was rarely reflected in the public media and was even less present in official reports to the Ministry of Overseas France (the new name, after the war, of the Ministry of Colonies). Thus through his teaching in class and his personal contacts Delavignette intellectually influenced the future overseas administrators.

What he told his students was well summarized in his *Les vrais chefs de l'empire* published in 1939. This book, clumsily butchered by the French wartime censorship, was reprinted in its entirety in 1946 as *Service africain* (four years later translated into English as *Freedom and Authority in French West Africa*). Much like *Paysans noirs*, it is an account of the life of the *commandants de cercle*, whom Delavignette argues are the real chiefs of the empire; but it is also a programmatic statement of the duties and responsibilities of the administrator. He is to exercise his authority the better to serve the people under his rule. He must respect the culture of the Africans but also bring to them the technology and gift for organization of the Western world. He must realize that the colonies are changing, moving away from their traditions and developing a new culture. The Africans who had had schooling in Western institutions and culture would be the new leaders of Africa; these earnest young men wanted to play a role in the new Africa that was developing. While it was common for many European administrators to scorn educated Africans, Delavignette welcomed them as the representatives of the new Africa. In Banfora in the late 1920s Delavignette had been friends with the young Voltaic schoolteacher of the town, Ouezzin Coulibally. He counted Léopold Senghor among his friends and in the book *Service africain* acclaimed him as the representative of the new emerging African man.

Service africain was a guide and program for future administrators; to those already in the field it was an articulation of their professional credo, spelling out the mission of the colonial administrator.[13] In his writings and teachings at ENFOM, Delavignette stressed French responsibility to the Africans and the need to understand their evolution by being in tune with the times. In this way, it has been argued, Delavignette prepared a generation of administrators to cope with decolonization.[14]

In 1946 Delavignette's directorship at ENFOM ended with his appointment as high commissioner to the Cameroons. The Cameroons had been a German colony until after World War I, when it had been partitioned by England and France. The despoliation of the German empire was done ostensibly to ensure better treatment for the peoples formerly ruled by Germany; these peoples were placed under the protection of the League of Nations with England and France appointed as "mandate powers." After World War II the United Nations, as heir to the League of Nations, established a trusteeship over the former mandate territories, and France was given trusteeship over its part of the Cameroons.

Like so much of the French empire the Cameroons had a sense of anticipation as the war ended. The Free French of General de Gaulle had for some time based their legitimacy upon their territorial control of part of the empire; they had also made heavy levies of resources and manpower which, it seemed, implied a debt of gratitude to the overseas people. In both the British and French empires the end of the war unleashed among the educated colonial elites a sense of a new era dawning. Many wanted independence; others insisted on at least enjoying equal rights with Europeans resident in the colonies. Neither the colonial administration nor the settlers living overseas, however, were cognizant of the profound changes in attitudes which had occurred as a result of the Second World War.

Frustrations of various kinds, including economic ones, beset a number of overseas territories, and the Cameroons was no exception. In the autumn of 1945 a series of violent demonstrations broke out. For the French government it was of particular importance that the mandate territories be governed with the minimum of friction; subject to international control, they were to be model territories. The appointment of Delavignette as high commissioner was intended to symbolize France's commitment to equitable rule.

The new commissioner had to appease the passions unleashed by the violent outbreaks of the autumn and to conciliate the white community, which was vehemently opposed to the new policy the Fourth Republic was introducing overseas of allowing some of the indigenous society to participate in political activities. He supervised elections held under the new constitution; he instituted new labor legislation abolishing forced labor and restrictions on labor union activity; he put into motion a new program of economic development. He had barely served a year when Marius Moutet, who again was minister, recalled him to serve as director of political affairs in the Ministry of Overseas France.

Delavignette came to the ministry at a time when it was facing its worst crises. Revolts against the French presence had broken out in Indochina in November 1946. The same kind of challenge to French rule had developed in areas that were not under the authority of the Ministry of Overseas France but were part of the empire (Algeria was under the authority of the Ministry of Interior, and Morocco and Tunisia were under the Ministry of Foreign Affairs). Stung by their humiliating defeat during the Second World War and by the German occupation, Frenchmen were adamantly opposed to retreating from their colonies. They saw such an act as an abnegation of national grandeur, confirmation of their loss of great-power status. Therefore it was very difficult for many Frenchmen to accept the process of decolonization, and they favored forceful repression of any challenges to their imperial dominance.

The violence in the colonies that accompanied opposition to French rule meant that French property and lives were endangered. The quite natural reaction of officials, whose first task was to preserve order, was to oppose such movements; Delavignette was no exception. The very day he became director of political affairs in the Ministry of Overseas France, revolt broke out in Madagascar. He sanctioned the attempt to reestablish order, an attempt that led to terrible excesses. His reaction to Malagasy nationalism was different from his later reactions toward other nationalisms in the French empire perhaps because he was intellectually unprepared for such a development. Elsewhere, in Indochina and North Africa for instance, important nationalist movements had already developed before World War II, and it was not difficult, therefore, to grasp what the nature of anti-French agitation was. In Madagascar, where there had been no such movements, the agitation could be more easily dismissed as a mindless outbreak of violence. It is also possible that Delavignette, faced by revolt on the very day that he took office, instinctively sought the restoration of order; preservation of order was the minimum expected of any colonial official.

In Indochina, however, Delavignette showed considerable sensitivity to the issues. Maybe this was because the evolution of a strong nationalist consciousness there was already well known in the 1930s. Unlike Madagascar, Indochina had been severed from France during World War II when the Japanese established control over it. Upon its defeat, Japan evacuated Indochina; during the interim before the French had a chance to return, the nationalist movement headed by Ho Chi Minh was established and claimed control over Vietnam. The French were at first ambiguous in their relationship to Ho, but very soon fighting broke out. Filled with illusions, French officials prosecuted the long colonial war hoping that some alternative to a Ho Chi Minh victory could be found.

One of the few officials who understood the extent to which the changes of the interwar era, the Second World War, and finally the Indochina war itself had transformed the colonial relationship was

Delavignette. In a series of courageous memoranda he explained to his
superiors that the Vietnamese wanted genuine independence. The relationship between Frenchmen and Vietnamese had become not unlike that
of Germans and Frenchmen in World War II. Attitudes had changed, and
the Vietnamese now saw the French as foreign occupiers. Delavignette
did not advocate outright abandonment of Indochina, but he clearly
pointed out the difficulty of the French insistence on remaining in their
Asian colony. The war in Indochina led to the transfer of French
policy-making from the Ministry of Overseas France to the generals in
Saigon and the Ministry of War in Paris. Thus the role of the overseas
ministry was diminished in Asia, and Delavignette's ideas had very little
influence. In any case Delavignette left the ministry in 1951 to return to
ENFOM as an instructor. His role as a policy-maker had ended.

Although no longer with the Ministry of Overseas France, Delavignette
was still very much concerned with the evolution overseas.
    He had never served in North Africa, but in the early 1950s he viewed
French policy toward that region with increasing alarm. In Tunisia and
Morocco nationalist opinion had made itself increasingly heard, and the
only French response had been repression. A group of French Catholic
intellectuals, led by François Mauriac, formed the Comité France-
Maghreb, which advocated negotiation with the nationalists and the
granting of some form of independence. Delavignette was a prominent
member of this committee.
    Many liberal Frenchmen could envision the independence of Tunisia
and Morocco; after all, they were legally protectorates. But Algeria was
a different matter: it was technically an integral part of France. Algeria
was considered fully assimilated to metropolitan France, although its
population was not. Neither in their political rights nor standard of living
did the Arab population of Algeria enjoy equality with the French settlers
in Algeria or the inhabitants of metropolitan France. The Arab population of Algeria had real grievances which easily were channeled into
nationalist agitation, especially since a similar mood had developed
in neighboring Morocco and Tunisia. On the night of November 1, 1954,
a small group of Algerian nationalists began the uprising that was to be
the Algerian war.
    Many institutions were to deal with the Algerian uprising. In the
summer of 1955 the Economic and Social Council, a high-level government advisory body, took up the Algerian question. Delavignette was a
member of the council and wrote its lengthy report spelling out the need
for a massive French commitment to achieve the social and economic
progress of Algeria. Implicit in the report was the notion that such a
pledge might avert the further spread of Algerian nationalism and that

failure to do so would spell the loss of Algeria. The proposals in the report could not be implemented, and the war spread in North Africa.

In an attempt to control the uprising, the French army instituted a police state in Algeria. The wholesale denial of human rights and the use of torture became so well publicized that in 1957, under considerable public pressure, the government appointed a Commission for the Protection of Individual Rights and Liberties to investigate the accusations made against the army and the administration in Algeria. Delavignette was appointed a member of the commission. He saw the commission as France's conscience in Algeria and was committed to the notion that the total truth would be most salutary to France's colonial mission. Anything else would poison the political system both overseas and at home. When he realized that the commission report would fail to clarify the extent to which the authorities in both Paris and Algeria had had prior knowledge of the use of torture and other illegal activities and were unwilling to right the abuses which had been committed, Delavignette resigned in protest. A year later the French army in Algeria, which had been virtually uncontrolled by the Fourth Republic, turned against the government and threatened an invasion of France if its Algerian policy were not adopted. The assumption of power by General Charles de Gaulle marked the end of the Fourth Republic but also averted civil war. The new French president decided that colonial issues had for too long diverted France from her domestic problems and her role as a power on the European continent. Therefore he favored an end to the war in Algeria (which came in 1962) and a process of decolonization in black Africa. In 1958 the constitution of the new Fifth Republic founded by de Gaulle gave the former colonies in black Africa a status akin to that of independence. By 1960 full independence was granted.[15]

While many administrators had difficulty adjusting to the changes occurring overseas, Delavignette welcomed them as ushering in a new era of full legal equality between France and her former overseas dependencies. He was eager to contribute no matter how modestly to the success of the newly independent states. In 1959 ENFOM had been converted to an administrative training school for African administrators, and Delavignette returned, as he had in times past, to teach the men who were to rule Africa.

With the end of the empire Delavignette attempted to put the whole imperial experience in perspective and wrote books and articles trying to sum up what French rule had meant both for Africa and the mother country. He also continued an old theme, the duty and responsibility of Frenchmen to their fellow human beings in Africa. Decolonization had not changed the fact that a richer, more technically advanced society had moral obligations to help those who were less well-endowed materially.

Nor was there any less reason to learn from African culture ethical values
and aesthetic perceptions that could enrich French civilization.

Insisting on the fact that the French have contributed to the history and
development of modern Africa, Delavignette was also instrumental in
the advance of French knowledge of Africa by spreading through his
writings both a sensitivity to the traditional aspects of Africa and
acquaintance with the new, evolving continent with its modern cities,
new universities, and ambitions for the future. Delavignette had seen in
the French empire an institution that affirmed the unity of men by
creating a symbiosis between various cultures. In the collapse of empires
built upon force he saw the opportunity of building new relationships
that would truly affirm the value of the universal, the human. Delavignette attempted to preserve and nurture the bonds which he had first
established with Africa over half a century ago; in 1974 he was still
corresponding with the chief of Banfora who had been village elder when
he had been the administrator there. He kept very much abreast of
current affairs in Africa, interrogating recent visitors on economic and
political developments. When drought hit the Sahel in the late 1960s and
early 1970s Delavignette was active in soliciting funds for aid to the
region. On February 4, 1976, aged seventy-nine, Robert Delavignette
died after a long illness.

He was one of the most notable members of the generation of
administrators to whom Maurice Delafosse, himself a distinguished
administrator, had applied the term *broussards*, that is, men who were
bush administrators, men who were as much African as European. By his
life and writings he had tried to exemplify this ability to span two
cultures.

While he had not set foot on African soil for the last twenty years of
his life, his thoughts often went to the continent. As old age advanced, he
thought of the men who fifty years earlier had been the village elders in
Niger and, using their manner of salutation, expressed his abiding wish
for Africa:

I send a Hausa greeting which I used to exchange with the old men.
It has lost nothing of its beauty and still has universal relevance:
"Peace! Lafia! How is the country? In Peace! Only Peace! Lafia Lo!"[16]

Notes to Introduction

1. Raoul Girardet, *L'idée coloniale en France* (Paris, 1972), 175–90.

2. Léopold Sédar Senghor, "Un gouverneur humaniste," *Revue française
d'histoire d'outre-mer* 54 (1967): 26.

3. Gaston Roupnel, *Histoire de la campagne française* (Paris, 1932). Auguste
Mairey, *Géographie générale* (Paris, 1911) and special texts on the colonies, *La
France et ses colonies* (Paris, 1902).

4. On the Barmou, where Delavignette served in 1923, see "Rapport politique 1er trimestre, Niger, 1923," Niger 2G23-24, Archives de l'Afrique occidentale française (henceforth cited as AAOF) Dakar. On Niger in general, see Sere de Rivières, *Histoire du Niger* (Paris, 1965).

5. Louis was Delavignette's middle name; Faivre was his mother's maiden name.

6. File 1C1069, AAOF.

7. The problem of census-taking in Africa is shown by the varying figures given for the subdivision of Banfora: in 1928 it was confidently given as 105,966 but a year later as 95,000.

8. "Haute Volta, Resumé du rapport politique annuel, 1928," Haute Volta, 2G28/15, AAOF.

9. "Rapport agricole annuelle, 1928, Haute Volta," 2G28/38, pp. 181–90, AAOF.

10. May 1932 note in File 1C1069, AAOF.

11. *Freedom and Authority in French West Africa* (London, 1950), p. 22.

12. Moutet letter in *Revue française d'histoire d'outre-mer* 54 (1967): 26.

13. Jean Claude Froelich, "Delavignette et le service africain," *Revue française d'histoire d'outre-mer* 54:44–51.

14. Pierre Kalck, "Robert Delavignette et la décolonisation," *Revue française d'histoire d'outre-mer* 54:52–64.

15. The exception was Guinea, which in a referendum in 1958 voted for full independence, while Somaliland opted to retain its former status as an overseas territory.

16. Robert Delavignette, "Souvenirs du Niger," *Revue française d'histoire d'outre-mer* 54 (1967): 21.

1　The District Officer

To rule its colonial populations overseas the French established a hier-archical bureaucracy having at its summit the minister of colonies, located in Paris, then his immediate representative, the governor-general, in charge of the two large administrative federations in black Africa: Afrique occidentale française (AOF), French West Africa, governed from Dakar; and Afrique équatoriale française (AEF), French Equatorial Africa, ruled from Brazzaville. Each federation consisted of several colonies ruled by a governor and, under him, smaller regional groupings known as *cercles*. The administrator in charge of the circle, the *commandant de cercle*, was the French equivalent of the British district officer. If the circle was unusually large, it was sometimes divided into subdivisions and the administrator heading the subdivision then had direct control over the local population, administering justice, levying forced labor to build local public works, collecting taxes, arbitrating between feuding groups, and performing numerous other functions which Delavignette describes.

The district officer's position entailed a double role; he represented France and at the same time might have to defend the local people from excessive arbitrariness from the bureaucrats in Paris or Dakar. As a government employee he had been taught to follow orders, but he also felt obligations to the local peoples which at times conflicted with his loyalty to his superiors.

Much of Delavignette's description of the bush administrator reflects rather well the dilemmas confronting the French official. Some of it is covered with a glow of idealization and should not necessarily be seen as an accurate reflection of the values held and accomplishments of all administrators. Nevertheless it is the most complete description given of the life of the *commandant de cercle* in the bush.

19

Asked in 1965 to speak on "The Territorial Administrator in French
Black Africa" by the French Academy of Moral and Political Sciences,
Delavignette gave an overview of the role and functions of the French
district officer (1). The many functions of the commandant were described
with great detail in the novel *Paysans noirs*, the history of twelve months
in the life of a fictitious district named Nerigaba, actually the subdivision of Banfora which Delavignette adminstered from 1928 to 1931.
One of the basic functions of the French official was to ensure his
control through the local chiefs. Their selection often presented serious
problems. In Banfora the minority Diola population had been used to
dominate the local Gouin peasants. French officials had abetted the Diola
domination, but a change of policy occurred and an effort was made to
encourage the Gouins to choose a chief from their own group. The
problems attendant on such a change of policy are depicted in the
selection from *Paysans noirs* (2). Not only ethnic strife, but even
generational problems could become the concern of the European
administrator intent on preserving the peace of his district (3). The
organization of local cash crop production was important, and the
administrator found himself in the role of intermediary—between the
European commercial houses and the African producers (4).

With so much responsibility the administrator had in his hands nearly
unlimited power; the danger was, of course, as Delavignette had warned
in his novel *Toum*, that the French official might become an autocrat.
Very perceptively he notes that this opportunity to exercise power was
one of the important attractions which led young men to choose the
profession (5).

Reflecting his desire to preserve his own power and his fear of the
danger to him and to Africa inherent in formal bureaucratic norms, the
bush administrator tended to view with hostility the upper echelons of
the colonial bureaucracy located in the colonial capital (6).

Far in the bush was the residency—the administrator's home and the
white man's castle in Africa, the last abode of men who had fled Europe
fearing its conformity and conventions (7). These residences had their
charms but they were also isolated from the surrounding population, and
there were times of loneliness and homesickness (8). The administrator
was the "European" in Africa and the "African" in Europe, never quite at
home anywhere, although one gets the impression that for the bush
administrator the residence came closest to being home (9). If Delavignette's presentation of the bush administrator was idealized, there
were times when he felt that all French officialdom was responsible for
the more somber elements of French colonialism such as forced labor. It
was remarkable in 1932 for a French colonial administrator to question
forced labor in the foremost colonial journal on Africa, *Afrique française*

(10). And it was just as unusual to be able to imagine how an African might view the strange ways of the white man living in their midst (11, 12).

Years after he had ended his service overseas and two years after the former colonies had become independent, Delavignette returned in his writing to the role and function of the district officer. He examined the motives and accomplishments of the colonial official and meditated on what his image had become in the postcolonial world (13). There were many disappointments on which retired officials could dwell, but some received encouragement from their continued contact with friends they had made in Africa, as is shown here in a letter written in 1974 from Banfora by Hema Fedma, who had been chief of the area nearly half a century earlier when Delavignette had been administrator (14).

1   The Territorial Administrator in French Black Africa

For more than half a century, from 1900 to 1958, French Black Africa comprised two general territories: French West Africa and French Equatorial Africa, to which were added in 1919 two territories under the mandate of the League of Nations (later under the trusteeship of the United Nations), Togo and the Cameroons. The total area was 18 million square kilometers—about thirteen times the size of France; and the population 28 million people, according to the 1955 census—two-thirds of the French population. The geographical dimensions were large but the density of population was very low. It was in this contrast between the vastness of the territory and the modest size of the population that the administration had to function. Do we have to remind ourselves that the administration was launched at the beginning of the century in huge countries hardly mapped? The African interior was organized around the districts. Under different names, circle, region, prefecture, the district was headed by an administrator, the permanent representative of the governor. The district was the collection of villages and counties [*cantons*]. If the number of villagers required it, the district was divided into subdivisions with an administrator at the head. Nothing was more diverse than the makeup of the 182 districts found in 1958 in French Black Africa. At times, the district seemed to be superimposed on a native province with which it shared the same boundaries; at other times it encompassed several of these provinces. Elsewhere, it was a cluster of villages which thus far had lived separately on their own. And I do not even touch on the subject of the Saharan borders where the nomadic way of life presented special problems. Because of its origin in conquest the district maintained a military appearance. That it was in a civil administrator's hands did not prevent it from still being connected with the notion of command. The African language expressed this very well: the administrator is the commandant.

Let us look at the bush administrator in the light of the difficulties which surround him during his required two-year stay. These difficulties can be classified into two large groups. First, let us consider those which come from his numerous bureaucratic duties. The district is similar to the traditional African community as far as its many functions are concerned. The district head resembles an African chief because he performs many functions. Paradoxically, direct administration leads to the administrator's Africanization. He presides over the court which rules according to local customs, if these are not opposed to the principles laid down by our civilization. The court is very often of his own making and he keeps it going as best he can. His decisions, taken in cooperation with native assistants, help form a new customary African law. Our bush administrator is responsible for taking a census. In AOF, out of the 111 existing circles in 1957, only 11 show a population density of more than thirty inhabitants to the square kilometer and 9 have less than one inhabitant to the square kilometer. Most have between three and thirty inhabitants per square kilometer. While taking the census, the bush administrator spends weeks camping from village to village.

He collects taxes. He works on the district's budget and public works organization. He is an accountant and a director just as he is a general officer and a judge. What responsibilities are not his? Later on, when the first technical commissions came to his districts, he played the role of what is today called a coordinator. On a regional level, it was his responsibility to see that the economic and social plan which encompasses the whole colony or a group of colonies is carried out. But during the trying period of the beginning, he was the pioneer in charge of many tasks. And until the end of the colonial era, he was the pillar of law and order.

Difficulties of the second type are those stemming from the populations whose mentality the administrator must know and whose reactions he must foresee. As he becomes more intimate with them, they reveal their stature, their faces, their importance, and their special charm. He feels himself, surrounded, penetrated, and carried by them. The districts with only one ethnic group, only one religion, are rare. In some of them, several dialects are spoken. In others, Islamism and Christianity are interwoven with ancient animism. And all of them represent a melting pot of races, where ancestral partitions crumble.

Peace brought by the French promotes trade and the coming and going of wealth and people. Former slaves are free. Around new cities, populations are milling. Even the requisition of workers—which the administrators loudly denounce—plays a part in the social mutation taking place in the district.

These working conditions are imposed on the territorial administrator, on the bush administrator. I did not speak of the sense of isolation and illness which threaten his physical and psychological equilibrium. The job requires a robust health which often is undermined in the performance of these tasks.

I now want to delineate in a few words the most difficult aspect of administering a district. On the one hand, the administrator is the Frenchman who tends to unify the different Africas through planning and through the civilization he represents. On the other hand, in order to fulfill his mission, he has to adapt to some faraway place in Africa and behave there as an adopted chief. He carries with him an ambivalence that borders on ambiguity. And Africa itself is ambiguous in its totality as well as in its districts. Africa is changing. And it is with this changing Africa that the bush administrator must keep in touch at all costs.

2   Choosing a Chief

The former African infantrymen entered, one by one, the large camp cabin where the white man had no other interpreter than Pertiou and no other white paraphernalia than a hurricane lamp. Upon hearing his name, the infantryman came running, his elbows close to his body, and bowed, already intimidated.

"Do you want someone from Bâ as a chief?" [said the commandant]

"Hon, Hon!"

"Or some wise man from a Diola family?"

"Hon, Hon!"

"Then who?"

"Ha—whoever you want. Nominate a lizard, we will obey it."

"I want you to give a man's name!"

"Ha!"

And the Gouin man squatted down, looking at the lamp and the ants running on the floor. With his hands tightly closed, he looked as if he were dividing a treasure into small piles. The commandant felt he had a day off and was playing cards in the village café with some of his peasant friends who pondered for hours before putting one card on the table.

"For God's sake, go ahead, I will keep it a secret."

"Then Kamon!"

This Kamon was one of Initima's relatives. Initima was the chief whom the commandant, in agreement with the young interpreter, favored.

Then the Diolas streamed in among the peasants or, more precisely, flanked by them. One Diola; two, three Gouins; one Diola. The minority was thus lost in the crowd.

Outside, the multitude was buzzing and coughing in the cool night. Children on their mothers' backs were crying. Guards were keeping an eye on the voters who had already cast their ballots to prevent them from talking to the others. The commandant could smell the peasants' sour body scent, so different from the Diolas', who used soap purchased in small shops. The Diola yelled from time to time: "Bokery Nian, Bokary, Ali's son." And the peasants were considering the same Gouin name: the old man is from Metiérédougou, a sorcerer and interpreter, Initima's relative. . . . And surrounded by an awful steam coming from their sweating armpits, they softly whispered in the commandant's ear: Kamon.

"I name Kamon!" cried the commandant when the election was over. The Diolas jumped quickly on their horses. Their long tunics floating, they flew away like night birds. Forms moved in the backs of trucks. Merchants were deploring the news. A Diola woman sneered: "He, the white man, chose a man with a ring. Oh, what a chief he'll make with a ring in his nose."

The commandant was taken to Kamon's cabin, escorted by the Gouins, who were amazed by their victory. Kamon, who had remained at home, did not seem surprised. He was a peasant. His lower lip was pierced in order to wear the ring which the Diolas mocked. (The young people did not follow this custom anymore because they were the objects of too much mockery.)

At Kamon's a celebration with millet beer and music took place. They lit a fire. Then old Kamon got up and started to dance. The Gouins rushed to join him while drums and bells were feverishly agitated. And the drum vibrated in the white man's belly—he was proud of having drawn Kamon's name out of the entrails of the Gouins.

3 Fathers and Sons

Many a young man who had worked hard in his future father-in-law's fields in order to get his sweetheart had to give up the idea of getting married to her. His old folks were holding onto his money and his fiancee's old father was asking for a bigger sum and was offering her to an old man. Thus the court never lacked cases. But children were born anyway. And some young lover—defying custom—would take woman and child to a chosen place where he would found a small, separate settlement.

In order to prevent such distressing situations, the commandant would often call the old folks and lecture them: "Why don't you keep your word! You already are spoiled by money. Who will cultivate the land next year if the young people are dissatisfied? Why do you burden me in such a way? I, who this year exempted you from paying taxes and forced labor."

Upon hearing this, the old men, all twisted, bony, hunchbacked, with hollow, worn-out faces and chests, who had come badly dressed but covered with bracelets, necklaces, rings, leather and bone charms, and carrying small keys around their necks (indicating that they had indeed bought tin trunks in which to deposit their money), would murmur words of submission through their teethless mouths, lower their eyes or show dead pupils, and raise their old chapped hands. And they would seem to say:

"All right, O white man, you have your peanuts, you have your share. Let us have our own share. Let us have our customs. Why do you always want something else and still something else? Why do you want to alter even our lives?"

Despite the attitudes of the old, the young people would still meet, choose, love, and want to marry one another. Young men would introduce the fiancees who had been promised them at plowing time. They would cry to the commandant: "Commandant, you saw how hard we worked in the fields. Today we are still working. We empty the small village granaries into the big CFCI* granary. We load the truck. We are repairing the roads. The old folks just watch and move only to get the white man's money. So they don't have our strength anymore. But why do they break up our engagements!" The interpreter would send them away. "Don't rebel against your fathers!"

But once, to everybody's astonishment, the commandant gathered not the old men but the old women and talked to them in a low voice, with his gaze lost in the distance: "O mothers, will you not do what is necessary so this country can be alive again? Only young people, well-matched and married, will produce life again. I trust you, O mothers who walk entirely naked as Eve did at the beginning of the world."

Afterwards, the old women left without a sound, not having exchanged a word—which also was a surprising event.

The old men chose then the oldest ones among them to be their representatives and sent a pleasing answer to the white man: "We will obey you, commandant. Let us first pay our taxes, then we will give our boys money to get married."

And the poet-sorcerers immediately said publicly: "Let the girls be happy with their lovers. Marriages will be performed as usual, after taxes

*The Compagnie française de la Côte d'Ivoire, one of the large French colonial companies (ed.).

are paid. This year, no girl will be given to an old man or will languish on her father's property."

And girls and boys were laughing, with youth's appetite for life.

4 Bringing in the Crop

The Europeans from the factory received their big boss who had thought of building the peanut oil press. Cost was discussed with the commandant.

"We cannot pay ten cents a kilo," asserted the CFCI boss. "The railway is still too far away from here. Our equipment has not paid for itself yet. And it is a bad year. Peanuts from Coromandel are flooding the market. The prices of commodities are falling all over the world."

Thus the Nérigaba peasants were caught in the big game. Through their efforts they had erected a factory in the depths of their continent. It was as if they had chartered a freighter that would carry their oil to Marseilles, Antwerp, Liverpool, Hamburg, with only the Master from the CFCI knowing its destination. It was as if they had converted their lands into stock.

"Firms are competing cent for cent," repeated the great boss. "We cannot afford to pay a cent extra."

He was not lying. The peasants who were harvesting the rest of the crop did not realize what an extra cent per kilo meant. But they too were caught up in the worldwide game. The boss was following the rules of the game. That is the way of the white man.

In order to protect somewhat the native producers, a system of sales was established. Twenty-seven villages along the roads were chosen, and four or five smaller villages that had no roads were joined to each of these twenty-seven. Each small village had to build one or several granaries in one of the villages on the road. Thus, no village was more than one day's walk from where crops would be sold. For we know that two walking-days mean failure. The peanut carriers reduce their load by taking food for the trip or by eating some of their crop on the way.

Every family head had to take his peanut crop to the granary in the village or neighborhood. He had to measure it by making notches on a reed, as old sharecroppers used to do. The white man says: "A cask is worth thirty cents, thirty. The notch represents ten casks, ten. It is fifteen francs, fifteen. That's more than the tax."

5 The Power of the Commandant

"One day," groans Commandant Benoiton, "a governor gives three hundred crowns to one of our colleagues and says: 'Here is some money.

Build me a post. Go!' " The colleague does what he is supposed to do; and when he is finished, my rascal of a governor comes to inspect. What awaits him is a nice stretch of road, a residency, with its out-buildings—a school, clinic, jail, shops, guards' camp, stables, garden, watering trough, courthouse, and he cries: "The wretched animal, all this for three hundred crowns; he took advantage of the natives and worked them to death!" The colleague answers coldly, "Who is most guilty: the governor who gives three hundred crowns to have a post built or the bush administrator who manages to accomplish what is asked of him?" The governor laughs and says: "After all, all the official vouchers have been satisfactorily filled out." Then he takes pictures which he sends to newspapers in France and for which he is congratulated.

"Yes," Commandant Labor goes on, "the governor knew very well that a thousand five hundred francs was not enough, but that was all he could spend, and the most important thing was to build the post. You are right, Benoiton, to retell this story. It shows that we can perform a task even if it is not quite legal and even if the governor may later judge it severely from his high position. It is an illustration of how we serve; we are fearless men who go straight to the assigned goal and find our rewards in the results we get. It is up to the higher-ups to choose and trust us."

"This is a job for dupes," says the gentleman.

"Young man," Commandant Labor says, "those who choose it for ambition or money or other worldly profit are dupes. Inadequate pay and bad reputation, this is the price paid for being in exile, working hard, being sick and alone. But let us proclaim it: almost all of us chose this job because we love it. Those who bitterly complain about it are those who are most devoted to it; they are consumed by a burning and corrosive love which brings them suffering but also rewards. And even those who perform dishonorably do so with a kind of loyalty, claiming vaguely the special nobility of the job. This is because it penetrates all the way to our bones and sharpens our personality to the utmost. However diverse the tasks it entails, whether it transforms us into a road surveyor or a judge, it always goes to our heads. All of us, boorish and refined alike, hear the same powerful call: Rule! It sends us into exile, it isolates us, it throws us in the heart of the bush country and then it deals with us. Men hesitate, discuss, or dream. They will rebel or become stupefied. But their calling whispers: 'Are you not white men? Don't you know what you are worth? We are counting on you: the natives are expecting you.' And lazy ones experience bursts of energy; stupid ones come up with a few smart ideas. What ruins everything, however, is the temptation to go too fast and the illusion that one can go beyond the limits of the possible."

6   What Is a District Officer?

He was always a man doing a demanding job, and he often lost his health in the process. He has been, for some years now, an overworked man who, like his natives strains the means he has at his disposal, means that are inadequate to fulfill the bureaucratic demands of the capital.

Would you like us to tell you bluntly what the vice of the administration is? The heads of offices work too, but these heads spend their time asking advice from the district officer—advice which materializes in reports, in papers.

For the native, the district officer is a chief whom one takes at his word. But for the staff of the governor, he is a civil servant whom one believes only on paper.

Should we go on? Should we say that within such a system, the prisoners' rations will be calculated with the utmost care, while the amount of forced labor being imposed is ignored? That the general secretary and the finance chief who sit next to the governor will receive in due time the invoices always signed by the same witnesses and by the district officer for the numerous illiterate people? That the papers will always be in proper form but that they will improperly express the true condition of the country? That the vocabulary about production increase will scrupulously follow the established -patterns but that the actual means of achieving increased production will be ignored? Trained by the colonial capital to follow formal rituals, forced to muddle through when faced by the native, the district officer, an overworked Janus, must have faith if he is to accomplish his mission. As for the governor, if he does not intuitively know the bush, if he does not have the bush administrator's trust and his own memories of what it was to be a district officer, he will claim that there is enough millet in his colony when a famine is ready to strike.

It is obvious that a change in the bureaucracy is needed. In fact, there is talk of ruling differently, more earnestly, with fewer offices, less red tape, fewer technical departments.

What is important? The natives. It is necessary therefore that the district officer be able to devote himself to knowing the natives and to communicating his knowledge to his superior.

7   The Residency: I

I have dreamed of the administrator's primitive residency. I have known it. Far away from modern Sudan and my native Burgundy, it was my home, the only one I ever owned.

A strange piece of property indeed. No family portraits, no family furniture. Comrades worked on it, not as if it belonged to them, but with other comrades in mind who would succeed them, and for me who would go on duty when my turn came.

Three rooms, all lined up along a hall, overlooked a circular porch with large windows which we closed with a straw shield during the heat of the day or a storm. A thatched roof sloped gently in the muggy Sudanese atmosphere, a terraced mud roof perched on faggots of brushwood, projecting over the African plain.

From June to October, the residency melted under the unceasing rain; from October to June, it was kneaded again by hand and baked once more in the sun. On days when the sun had been a blazing fire, the residency blinded me, and at night it made me sick. I would go and sleep far from its walls, which choked me.

The furniture was either made of local wood or of crates on which you still could read: "Fragile-Administration-Bordeaux." I am told that wardrobes with mirrors are now available. Then the great luxury was a cemented shower; cement was more expensive than sugar.

The white man did not pay attention to the bats that were mating as they flew and bumped against the ceiling and the walls; he ignored the mason flies that swelled the walls with their blister-shaped nests and the swallows that stuck theirs on the beams. He protected himself against termites by putting the wardrobe feet in oil-filled tin cans.

He never looked into the kitchen, which was outside the house and concealed what is most French in the country: an oven for baking bread.

You did not work there, you visited. Sparse shrubs, like greasy and extinguished tapers, surrounded small mounds of mud. Commandants whose deaths had stretched their visits through eternity, lay there with their domestics, guards, and translators. In a country where it is not customary to build visible tombs, this cemetery constituted one of the most European features of the residency.

Sometimes, a child born of two races laughed. It most probably would be on the Fourteenth of July, when his mother, a deserted Sudanese woman, came to the residency to beg, carrying or dragging the child whose color would differ from that of everyone else.

Before brunettes and blondes came in great numbers, the mistress's role was played by black or Fulani women. Their beautiful bodies, either ebony- or copper-colored, with slightly skinny, undersized calves and long thighs, with shoulders and neck sculptured by daily burdens carried on their heads, were part of a very sensuous Sudan: their presence gave life to the residency for a long time.

The presence of the women was indispensable but yet unfulfilling, and bitterness crept into these relationships. The fact that they were easy to get left one with the feeling of having failed. The white man was not fathering a new race. And did he really know his African "wife"? He did not recall easily his companion's face, which was associated with certain

residencies where only events from the past week constituted the core of
life. He could not tell the color of her eyes; maybe they were blue. He
would have been unable to depict her round forehead, the shape
emphasized by her abundant, wooly hair put up in a crest. He barely
remembered her purple, generous mouth visible under her large nostrils.

White women call the moussos toward whom they feel jealousy:
"blood sausage skins!" But their feeling should be directed instead against
the residency, for it was one of the last castles where man could find and
enjoy solitude.

8   The Residency: II

Our residency combined not only the rooms of our humble lodgings and
our office but also the "telegraph," the jail (prisoners were often servants,
and I have known commandants who were attended by them when sick),
the court house, the guards' camp, the millet granaries (in case of crop
shortage) the vegetable garden, the school, a shop, the clinic, then the
chapel of the missionaries, and, one fine day, the railway station, which
was the last stop from the coast.

There, we performed ancient tasks: we counted families and herds and
built roads. There, we collected taxes and presided over justice. We
wrote monographs about the district we lived in (and if these had been
gathered and bound, they would have constituted moving evidence of
what we knew of Africa). There, we had good cooks and we got together
with friends to share colonial dishes concocted in frying pans full of
grease. There, hospitality and friendship were freely given.

And we hung onto the mail coming from France, the news written by
the families or our sweethearts. We read the newspapers from cover to
cover, including advertisements, as well as books that Frenchmen short
of time no longer read. We read precious letters over and over again. We
dreamed about France. We lay motionless in the grip of a terrible fever.
There, we learned about a mother's death.

Behind the guards' camp, there was our cemetery. Guards and
interpreters considered it an honor to be buried there. And it is there that
I saw the most inviting trees in the world.

A danger lay at the core of this life. And the danger was its very
charm. The commandant was surrounded by a strange castle, in a
strange land, with a strange servant-mistress. He sometimes fell under
the spell. Every morning, he took a walk in his yard and at night he
worked over his papers and files in his office.

But around him a silent conspiracy was being erected by the interpreter, the guard-officers, the chiefs' representatives, the chiefs themselves and their vassals. Very slowly, he was losing his grip on the

African land, and families, the real representatives of the land, seemed to
turn away from him as they were greeting him. He had to make an
unending effort to get in touch with them again by rediscovering himself.

9 Nostalgia

Memories of evenings in Niger come to my mind, evenings during which
I would be happy just by reading my department's newspaper. Ah! The
dear newspapers, almost as precious as a parent's or a friend's letter! In
order to come and tell me its stories, it had to make the never-ceasing
journey: it would sail the ocean, land on the pier, go beyond the lagoon,
get into the small train which looked like a toy compared to the
enormous continent, and then, at the last station, go by pack-animal, as
we said over there, and ride on camel-back. I know very well that
modern tourists go faster, but that was in the old days, and in many
small places the old days still exist.

Whether in a bush village, at the halting-place or in a small fort, a kind
of a compromise between a Vauban-like fortress and Negro sultan's
palace, the residency always loomed in the savannah as a lifelong home,
as I read and reread the local news and the ads. They were one or two
months old and, even had they been recent, you would have found them
very bland, but to me they were sparkling with freshness and strangely
beautiful. The thefts of rabbits, the Polish worker without legal papers,
the college graduation day, the forestry official's death, the wedding of
the butcher's daughter, the birth of Peter, Paul, and James, the wheat
harvested, the hay newly mown—you cannot imagine how meaningful
all these news items were to me. The ads for furnished rooms for rent,
houses for sale—what wholesome adventure novels they brought me!
And the restaurants, the fine cuisine from my native country. How I was
looking forward to tasting those dishes when my local cook, lighting the
hurricane lamp for dinner and shouting "Here is the next course!"
brought me the skin-and-bone chicken and warm wine. O Sudanese
nights! I would have been as unable to withstand your wild and
star-studded splendor as to bear the overpowering heat of the day, if I
had not been able to relax and regain equilibrium by reading the trivial
news items in the paper of my native land and by delighting myself with
a sense of loneliness renewed by this reading.

And now that I am in Paris, I get the same pleasure, I draw the same
strength, out of the colonial newspapers. They keep me informed about a
way of life which was mine, which still exists and which spreads more
and more. They tell me that a kilo of Danish butter costs 22 francs and
that the Abidjan band played the "Marseillaise" and "Tipperary" on the
Fourteenth of July.

10   A Quote from Taine

I am somewhat bitter and sad as I force myself to recall some of my
memories. Most of the Upper Volta administrators were generous,
honest, hard-working, and I know governors whom I will always recall
with affection and respect. Nevertheless, how could I explain that 500,000
natives had to toil in order to support 300 Europeans! Why do I intuitively think that a fundamental mistake was made? In the Volta Club
library, at Ougadougou, there was Taine's *History of English Literature*. I am haunted by a quote in it from Macaulay. I recall this
much: "I give you proof that he was a bad king and you tell me that he
was a good husband, a good father, and a man of the world!"

11   The Ways of the White Man: I

The commandant was asking more and more questions from Pertiou,
Initima, and from whoever was willing to talk.

"What are the people who dig with a pick doing?"

"They are harvesting spring peanuts."

"And these women with their children all seated around a fire in the
field?"

"They are shelling spring peanuts."

"And why this pile of grass?"

"It's compost to be used in the field next year."

"Why are you smiling?"

"This is a Caraboro's field."

"And then?"

"Caraboros did not use to work, but the Gouins and the Turkas made
fun of them this year."

"And these people who are carrying baskets full of garbage?"

"It's the dump from cabins that will manure next year's fields."

"Who taught you this?"

"It's customary to do so here, and the former commandant, Ferriol,
advocated it too."

"And over there where the cattle is grazing, wasn't that once a field?"

"Yes."

"And this tam-tam?"

"It is the young people who are threshing the fonio in the village chief's
yard."

"And this?"

"It is this."

"And that?"

"It is that."

"Why are you laughing?"

"I am not laughing, Sir."

12 The Ways of the White Man: II

"In the middle of the courtyard stands a large building on top of which the French flag is waving: it is called the office. There the gentleman sits. There, you will go. In the back, there is the jail."

"And what is this office?"

"Don't be frightened; this house of authority is the paper house. You will see the white man bent over a table, a pen in his hand. He uses and makes papers for everything. Papers for us, our fields, our herds, our wells, our villages, our tales; papers for births and deaths; papers for the rain; papers for the grasshoppers. Give him money for taxes or fines, he will give you back a piece of paper. Papers with one, two copies, papers written with inks of different colors, filled with seals and signatures. And all these pieces of paper are sent on camels' backs to Damagaram where pen-pushers reread them, cross out words, make many copies. Then they go on by car, railways, and boats to the country where white men live; once there, new pen-pushers glue them together and give them ceremoniously to old men as high-grade food. White men are the paper people.

13 The Commandant in Perspective

Our uniqueness lay in the paradox that we were both the agents of the French central government in the African world and the agents of the African world confronted by the mother country's government and its colonial agencies. To a certain extent, the prefect, too, is the representative of his department and of a province faced by the centralizing powers of Paris. Sometimes he sides with his local council, but most often he fulfills his mission best by reconciling local interests with those of Paris. But we were more profoundly marked by the land where we lived than a prefect is. We symbolized a power that was very ambivalent and thus not without ambiguities. This ambivalence made it possible for us to defend our populations against our superiors by interpreting in their favor the freedom of action we had and the abstract principles which they ordered us to implement in lands whose human aspects they would have ignored if it had not been for us.

More so than the province administrator of the old regime and the prefect inherited from Napoleon by the succeeding governments, we had to be lonely and active chiefs who gained a deep knowledge about African countries which no headquarters could understand as well as we did; we also had to respond personally to the inner truth of these countries, as if we had sensitive antennae, and we consequently had to adapt rules and memoranda sent to us by governmental agencies. Above all, we had to defend all the way up to headquarters the rights of the African natives.

But we must confess that, despite the legal principles which are respected in the mother country, we had too much power in our hands and that we might consequently have suffered from slight corruption. For, as everyone knows, power corrupts and absolute power corrupts absolutely.

Thanks to the men in the bush, an entity at first bureaucratic, colonial, and artificial did take root in the African soil, and the grouping of these districts formed a territory which became the object of African patriotism.

I am aware of how difficult it is to describe us, the men in the bush. One way to accomplish this would be to explain what the mother country did not understand about us. In her opinion, we were merely jacks-of-all-trades. We were seen in the same manner in which sedentaries greet the swagger of some exotic adventurer; we were looked at with the indulgent smile the sedate bourgeois gives to the Bohemian artist. But such a portrait amounted to a caricature. Yes, we were jacks-of-all-trades since we had to read rain precipitation levels as well as collect African traditions. We were also jugglers since we had to build roads with little money, and we were like circus people in that we were always willing to accomplish the most unexpected tasks. Finally, we did not shun the adventure of catching malaria, sleeping sickness, and yellow fever. The reward many of us received still was, around 1920, an official tomb in some bush cemetery.

Our true originality is still difficult to grasp. We were not representatives of a high social class as some British colonial administrators or Dutch patricians might have been. We came from middle-income families where most members were minor civil servants. Whatever our social origins, however, we shared a common calling which, diverse as it might have been in its expressions, sprang from the same spirit.

Our originality remained also unnoticed by the crowds who lived indiscriminately in the cities that we had deserted for the bush; in fact we looked very outmoded to them.

But what kind of men were we really? Were we autocrats, oligarchs? These words encompass vastly more than our lives, which were made up of humble tasks, humble cares, and humble assignments. "Your bush administrators," the politicians told me, "do not know how to seek favors in political circles." He was referring to the first parliamentary assemblies in Africa. No, they only knew how to make tours during which they took census of their populations and presided over tribunals. They were not courtesans, even less demagogues. And they were bound to be left alone. Forgotten by the new African world whose birth they had prepared, they have nothing more to do now except drink the bitter cup which consists not of being denounced by anticolonialists but of being glorified by conservative colonial minds that do not even begin to understand their true grandeur.

14   Letter from an Old Acquaintance

Banfora, 29 July 1974

Dear Mr. Robert Delavignette,

I received your letter as well as the two copies of *Paysans noirs* with great joy. My two young relatives to whom I gave them were overjoyed.

We know that you are deeply attached to the building of our dear country, since you insisted that a ship bear the name of my village, which is Banfora.

In 1951, this ship was the first one to dock at Abidjan, where I was at the time a member of the Upper Volta delegation. I have had the great honor and the time to visit this beautifully built ship from top to bottom. This ship was proof that you are deeply attached to the construction of our beautiful country.

The two young relatives to whom you sent the book want me to thank you profusely for the noble deed you accomplished.

Only old age prevents you from coming back to visit this country which remains in your mind as vividly as your own family. No one here has forgotten your name of Commandant *Tchidjan*.* The old ones have all passed away.

I stop now and give to you and your family our warm and sincere thanks.

Very Sincerely,

Hema Fedma
Canton Chief BP2
Banfora

Tchidjan means "big one," an appropriate enough nickname for the tall-framed Delavignette (ed.).

Sources

1. "L'administrateur territorial en Afrique noire française," *Revue des travaux de l'académie des sciences morales et politiques* 118 (1965): 83–89.
2. *Paysans noirs* (Paris: Stock, 1931), pp. 63–67.
3. Ibid., pp. 160–68.
4. Ibid., pp. 145–47.
5. *Toum* (Paris: Bernard Grasset, 1926), pp. 257–60.

6. "La Réorganisation de l'Afrique équatoriale française," *Afrique française* 44 (1934): 390–94.

7. *Soudan-Paris-Bourgogne* (Paris: Bernard Grasset, 1935), pp. 61–65.

8. *Afrique occidentale française* (Paris: Editions géographiques et maritimes, 1931), pp. 66–67.

9. "La vie quotidienne et les feuilles locales," *Journal des debats*, August 13, 1933.

10. "Une nouvelle Colonie: D'Abidjan à Ouagadougou," *Afrique française* 42 (September 1932): 528–29.

11. *Paysans noirs*, pp. 112–21.

12. *Toum*, pp. 73–74.

13. *L'Afrique noire française et son destin* (Paris: Gallimard, 1962), pp. 41–50.

14. Copy of letter from Hema Fedma, Banfora, July 29, 1974, to Robert Delavignette. Delavignette Papers, Archives nationales, section outre-mer, Paris.

2

The Training
of Colonial
Administrators

Originally the colonial service was recruited haphazardly, with little concern for the qualifications of the men appointed overseas. It was hard enough to attract men to go to the colonies much less to pose conditions for their appointment. Thus the early administrators consisted of a motley group of men, mainly military personnel, explorers, minor clerks already serving overseas, and functionaries from metropolitan France. In 1889 the Ecole coloniale was founded to train future administrators; but it was not until after World War I that attendance at the school became a prerequisite for appointment. Until then only about a fifth of the colonial administrators were graduates of the Ecole coloniale; the rest continued to come from various sources.

The change which occurred in 1920 signalled a new era in the history of the school: it now had the monopoly on recruitment for the entire Corps of Colonial Administrators. The history of the school, its gradual development, its curriculum and philosophy, were outlined by Delavignette in 1937 when, as director of the Ecole nationale de la France d'outre-mer (the new name of the school), he attended an international congress in Holland to discuss the training of overseas administrators (1). Delavignette avers that the graduates of the Ecole coloniale (the school was known as the "Colo" and its graduates as "Colos"), through their study of overseas societies and peoples, were in the forefront of those discovering the nature of non-European societies (2). As director and teacher at the school, Delavignette developed a pride in his institution and its students. His affection for the young men is reflected in the loving memoir he sketches of those who attended the school in the dark years of the German occupation. He ends the memoir by stressing the importance of the role of the school beyond the colonial era—as an example to the independent ex-colonies (3).

1   The Colonial School

This school that opens up the world is located in a place which is pleasing to the sedentary philosopher. It calls to passionate youth to board for Africa and Asia, Madagascar and the islands of the Pacific. And it seems that the school chose to exalt traveling and exoticism by its location amid the well-trimmed trees of the avenue Observatoire, a classical setting that could not be surpassed for reminding a man of the spirit and grandeur of his own country. It is as if, before sending its graduates to faraway lands, the school wanted them to take with them the memory of a well-land-scaped courtyard. Before the baobab and the bamboo, here are the Luxembourg chestnut trees; before the bush and the jungle, the old, straight trees.

Everyone is aware that the aim of the school is to train young Frenchmen for the colonial administration. But, it is generally not known that it was built, some fifty years ago, to teach the natives about the mother country.

The school first consisted of a delegation of thirteen young Cambodians sent to Paris in 1886 in order to assimilate our civilization. This delegation took lodging on rue Jacob and later on rue Ampère. In 1888 the original school was transformed into the Ecole coloniale and installed on boulevard Montparnasse by Paul Dislère, councillor of state, section president of the Council of State. In 1896 he also had the buildings on avenue Observatoire erected with private donations and loans. For about forty years, everything was in his hands. From 1889 to 1928, when he was succeeded by Governor-General Roume, Paul Dislère, as president of the school's council of administration, was the great master of the school he founded. With the help of the succeeding directors, Aymonnier, Doubrère, and Max Outrey, and of Mr. Jourda, the secretary-treasurer, he watched over the school; he fixed its budget and its curriculum; he built up the library. On Sundays he wrote down the students' grade averages.

The natives no longer are part of the student body. The last ones left in 1913, and their section was closed in 1927. The task now is to train administrators for the nascent empire.

Paul Dislère was expert in the legal aspect of the empire. He was the lawmaker who set the colonial training within the boundaries of the law. He wrote a treatise on colonial law and trained men who would follow it.

By 1927, the school was well established and could undergo a major transformation. This was carried out by the minister of colonies, Léon Perrier, with the collaboration of the inspector of public education, Paul Crozet, and the work of a new director, Georges Hardy. Hardy was a graduate of the Ecole Normale, a disciple of Lavisse, a historian and a geographer; in short he is the Georges Hardy you all know. He comes from Dakar and Rabat. He gave the school a more pronounced academic bent while insisting on a more diverse and more concrete colonial curriculum. He recruited students directly from high schools through competitive examinations. He opened the school's windows on other fields which are necessary to a colonial administrator in his many assignments. The school had been built on a sturdy pillar of law. Now it could expand into other fields.

During the two periods that can be broadly characterized as the legal and the academic, the school acquired the structure and shape which it still possesses today. We will examine it quickly.

There are four sections: (1) the administrative section; (2) the trainees' section; (3) the magistrates' section; (4) the section which prepares candidates for the administrative examinations for North Africa.

1. The administrative section forms the bulk of the school, that is to say 75 percent of the student body, or 143 students at the beginning of the 1936 school year. Let us note immediately that the buildings were erected forty years ago for about fifty students. Now it has to take in almost two hundred, all sections included. The administrative section must turn out student-administrators for the overseas territories and for the Indochinese civil services. The section is therefore divided into two subsections: one dealing with Indochina, the other with Africa and Madagascar. After the first year, the students may choose the program they will study for the following two years. At the end, the students get the school diploma and a post as student-administrator.

Students are recruited through competitive examinations. Preparatory sections for these examinations are found [in secondary schools at the following locations]: Louis-le-Grand, where three sections had to be opened; at Chaptal; and outside Paris in Bordeaux, Marseilles, Toulouse, and Grenoble. Every year the number of candidates varies between 320 and 400 for about 40 positions. There are three parts to the written examination: French composition; French colonial history; general geography. In 1939, a fourth will be added: *moral** and sociology. The oral part of the examination consists of these subjects plus geology, botany, zoology, a foreign language, and also a law test for those who do not have the certificate one gets after the first year in law school.

The originality—and the difficulty—of such an examination is that it requires two types of preparations: one at the lycée and the other in law school. And the difficulty does not end with the examination. The successful candidates are now students and must go on with their legal studies which terminate with the *licence* in law. Sometimes, intoxicated

*This is a French subject which might best be translated as "situation ethics" (ed.).

with the intellectual prospects of Parisian places of learning, our young
men would like to take courses at the Sorbonne, the School of Oriental
Languages and the Institute of Ethnology. I do not reject this exalted
curiosity, this desire for total knowledge, for it reveals youth and
nobility of mind; but it also points to a certain danger—the school might
no longer be the focus of its own students' lives.

Part of the school's teaching is in fact a prolongation of the lycée, part
the formation of administrators. Thus, there is on the one hand a general
culture to be acquired and on the other a professional training. We will
discuss this subject further when we have examined all the different
sections of the school.

2. The trainee section was created in 1913 and reorganized in 1921 and
1926 on the basis of a competitive examination. The goal is to sift, by
means of an examination in French and in political economy, the best
candidates amid the lower French officials and clerks of French West
Africa, French Equatorial Africa, the Cameroons, and Madagascar.
Usually, there are about twenty openings for one hundred or so
candidates. The successful candidates go through a training period at the
school; hence their name of trainees. This period corresponds to a short
school year, starting in November and ending at Easter. If, after their
studies, they pass the final examinations, they get a diploma allowing
them to become administrators. They go back to the colonies where they
will encounter former graduates from the administrative section.

Thanks to the recruitment of trainees, the school opens its doors to
young men whose vocation has led to several stays in the territories
overseas and who already have intellectually matured through their
positions of command. Furthermore, we are dealing with civil servants
who come with a university degree and whose general culture is as broad
as the one required to get into the administrative sections.

3. The section for magistrates was founded in 1905. Candidates have
to take a competitive examination and should already have a degree in
law; their schooling lasts two years. Students should be assured of an
immediate position, as is the case for the graduates of the two previous
sections, but unfortunately there are very few posts. Since we cannot be
sure that the students would not have to wait for a vacancy, we have
decided to stop giving the examination.

4. Finally, there is a very special section, that for North Africa,
founded in 1924. Students are not recruited through competitive examinations but are chosen by the school's administrative council. Here they
are prepared for the competitive examination required of those who want
to become civil controllers in Tunisia and Morocco and junior administrators in Algeria. The curriculum lasts two years.

This review of the different sections of the school shows its complexity and its expansion, an expansion which parallels that of the colonies themselves. This is even more noticeable if we analyze the school with respect to its curriculum. We distinguished two great periods: the Dislèrian, or legal, era followed by what we called the academic period. It seems that we are approaching a third period in which the school will rely more and more on the university, while opening itself up more to the colonial realities and acquiring the characteristics of an applied institute.

Some may wonder if colonial *methods* really exist. According to these people there are only *processes*, which do not have to be taught in school; they simply have to be transmitted from generation to generation, each generation contributing the necessary changes for adaptation to time and place. However, colonial studies are diversified; this diversity is due to the nature of the colonizer and the colonized, to the different mother countries and their colonies; and colonial realities can vary with time for the same mother country and the same colony. Fears of a doctrine, at least fear of a doctrinal mind, can be felt. But we have been witnessing for a few years already, in Black Africa as in North Africa, in Asia and in the Indian peninsula, tremendous work being done on comparative colonization, work which is anchored in reality and crosses national boundaries. Thanks to contact with realities and to the lack of ideology, successful experiments with colonial processes are numerous enough for us to rightly talk not about process but about method: important problems are being viewed in the same way, and coordination of administrative experiences is taking place; experiments in the colonies have nothing to do with preconceived ideas but are based on research on the ethnological and sociological characteristics of the natives. Something new has happened: colonial questions are no longer subject to polemics but to critical knowledge based on scientific studies of comparative colonization and experimentation. This is enough to justify the foundation of colonial schools and to determine their orientation.

How does the school respond to the necessity of colonial experimentation? With, as I said before, a broad curriculum and a professional one. The broad curriculum suitable to future colonial administrators is based on several subjects on which everyone is in agreement. They are the history of colonization, the geography of colonial countries, the ethnology, linguistics, and sociology of the overseas peoples and law.

The professional teaching is still subject to much debate. Everyone agrees that the sciences of administration should be foremost. If anyone should know how the colony is organized, it is of course the administrator. Some would like to add an encyclopedic curriculum to the administrative sciences, but we should be cautious here. What do we want to do? Not form specialists in all problems which can arise in a district, a circle, a province, but train administrators who can exercise authority on all the sections of their territories. The spirit inherent in the administrator's job does not change, although the ways of doing it evolve. Our young men who will be in the corps around 1940 will not be performing exactly the same tasks as their elders before 1900. Today's administrator is surrounded by agronomists, engineers of public works, school teachers, doctors and veterinarians. He does not have to compete for knowledge with these technicians; he does not have to put his authority at stake in each field. On the contrary, he must know enough to respect specialization so as not to hinder the true specialist. It is this perspective that we must inculcate in him as soon as he enters the school. The administrator's professional curriculum should not be a hodgepodge of different specialties but should lead the student to a general knowledge of these specialties.

And here we should realize that the relationships between the administrator and the technician are of paramount importance and that, if they are not harmonious, the whole colony suffers *through its natives*. The administrator represents authority for the natives, and it is the natives that the technicians need and will use. Whether in laying out a road, cultivating a new plant, opening a school, vaccinating a population, the technical problem is linked to a human problem. And it is to this human problem that the administrator must find a solution. The technicians expect him to show them the one technique that is his own: knowledge of the natives.

The administrator's technique is not based on encyclopedic knowledge but on a double concept: what is legal, and what is humanly feasible for the natives. The first can be taught at the school through the study of administrative sciences; the other is more a feeling which can only be awakened at the school through the study of native countries and peoples.

Knowledge of the law and of the native enables the administrator to perform his tasks and make his command possible. The ability to command is a very specific aspect of the administrator's duty. The colonial administration possesses a power to command of a higher degree than that of the mother country. For, over there, there is between the administrator and the people under his jurisdiction a chasm in life-style and thought which can only be bridged by the exercise of experienced and humane authority. The most important problems facing the colonial administration directly concern men and cannot be solved simply through the application of law but belong rather to the domain of ethics. It is then that the moral role of commanding appears as a glaring necessity, a necessity which is hard to imagine in Europe.

This authority requires a resolute faith in the humanity of the native populations as well as a flexible method which studies their character and takes their personalities into account. This style of authority has a value which is ignored by people who prefer that of [a more regular] government which appears loftier and less accessible. In the French empire, more than sixty million men live under such rule, and their progress as well as their outlook depends as much on governments as on colonial rule.

This is why we want to make a laboratory out of this school. We are not trying to sacrifice a broad curriculum in favor of a professional one. No, there is not one technique which does not become routine if it does not originate in a broad culture always in the process of renewal. A mind is not a good mind, in the Cartesian meaning, if it is not put to good work. And applying what one has learned is not the least important part of the school's education.

Whether dealing with a broad curriculum or a professional one, we must be careful about scholasticism in our students, about passive minds and bookishness. We must look to the real world with which students will come into contact, in field trips, for example. By becoming a practitioner, dare I say a "clinician," the administrator really grasps what his functions are and contributes to the knowledge of geography and history, of ethnology, sociology, linguistics, administrative sciences and law; in a word, to the knowledge of those subjects which marked him at the school. We want the student to start thinking like the administrator he will become and to absorb into his class notes the rules of the profession. Without this, diplomas would be nothing but worthless pieces of paper.

Our students will take their most difficult examination far from their teachers, elsewhere in the world. Those who will grade them will do so silently and definitively. They will be the people under their jurisdiction, the natives. They will judge whether or not we have formed men able to lead other men.

2 "Colo" and Science

Among all the graduates from this school, first named "Colo," then ENFOM, who went to Black Africa or Madagascar, how many realized that the science of man could give significance to their colonial lives and that it would permeate the whole administration to which they belonged? None of the personnel officers whose task was to assign some to the bush, others to the colonial capitals, could guess that this judge would be an ethnologist, this administrator a linguist or a historian. Some at the beginning of their careers, others as they went on, discovered a new calling, committed themselves to scientific research. And this is still going on. The "Colos" have left their diverse administrative posts but they still work in the social sciences to whose progress they have contributed so greatly.

Some people claim that a civil servant—whether a judge, an administrator, a labor inspector—could not be a researcher. We assert the opposite view and claim that the spirit of science manifests itself where it wants to. What was needed first was a feeling of empathy towards Africa and Africans, towards Malagasy people and Madagascar; to my knowledge, the Colo was not lacking such a predisposition. Then an intellectual discipline specific to each specialty was required, and the Colo acquired it despite numerous difficulties set up by the bureaucracy in which he worked. Finally, he needed free time, for, contrary to myth, he often was overworked. But while on duty the Colo found countless opportunities to carry out research. Working with natives allowed him to inquire quite naturally about their behavior and mores and permitted him to immerse himself in the same physical and moral milieu. History, ethnology, sociology, linguistics, customary and comparative law benefited tremendously from these trips in the bush, these outdoor court sessions, these census operations, all performed by Colos on the spot.

Personally, I will add that while looking for African or Malagasy man, the Colo did believe in this man at a time when the mother country did not. To search for man is to believe in man. This African, this Malagasy was illiterate. And to the mother country, illiterate men were only savages or overgrown children. By searching for man, believing in man, the Colo was fighting against prejudices. The traditional image which supported the mother country's sense of superiority over Africa and Madagascar gave way only when scientific research done in Black Africa and in Madagascar won university approval. The Colo had done his share.

3   The School in the Dark Years

To think in "imperial" terms in an occupied France during the winter of 1943–44 was not, for this community of future colonial administrators, to think in terms of dominating the overseas world which they were so eager to know and for which no sacrifice was too great. One of them wrote to me in 1943: "It will be more difficult than ever to defend our empire because it will have to be reconstructed. Such a reconstruction will not only be material but also spiritual. We have to give the rest of the world proof that France is still capable of sacrificing herself to high ideals." Did this young man for whom the empire had to be rebuilt and whose calling was to serve people have a vision too large, too beautiful, too generous?

The answer should be no, since many of his classmates shared such a vision. Some students brought up in "the atmosphere of faith and intellectual freedom" characteristic of the school, chose to become shadow soldiers, to join Resistance groups in occupied France or to enroll in the Free French Army. One of them had this note handed to me: "I am sure you have not forgotten those among your students who have gone to North Africa via Spain. I am happy to tell you that, in the Italian campaign as well as in front of Toulon, we gave proof to our infantrymen as well as to our superiors that we had learned the great teachings of the school." Another wrote before joining the Resistance, where he was eventually to be shot, "I simply want you to know that I am leaving to serve as a Frenchman."

How can we forget you, young men with youthful faces but ready to accomplish manly tasks and give up your lives? How can we not think of all of you as one community, those who fell in 1914–18 and in 1939–45 on all fronts, including Indochina and Algeria, and those who died while serving in the overseas territories? I will name only one since I cannot name them all: he is the last one on the alphabetical list of those killed in 1939–45: Vieillard. Gilbert Vieillard.

I am informed that he was killed at the end of June 1940, a few days after the armistice; he was still fighting in Lorraine, near Vaucouleurs. He had been adopted as one of their own by the Fulani, in whose country he had been an administrator.* Upon his death they founded in Guinea the association of Gilbert Vieillard's friends. He had lived the words uttered by one of the school founders, Auguste Pavie, the postal official and explorer of Laos: "I have experienced the joy of being loved by the peoples among whom I passed," and he had done so in his own way, as an ethnologist-administrator.

And among the shadow soldiers, I would like to mention at least two: Maurice Buhler and Bernard Maupoil. Buhler was arrested on April 21, 1944, at the Saint Lazare station, tortured—but did not speak—deported, and assassinated on July 2, 1944; Bernard Maupoil, veteran of the International Brigades that fought in Spain and devotee of the African theater, was shot down on February 15, 1944, in Paris. I have reason to believe that, if Buhler and Maupoil had talked while being tortured, the list of the Colos arrested by the Gestapo would have been longer still.

On August 24, 1944, a former student, the administrator Raymond Dronne, who had left the Cameroons in order to be a captain in the Leclerc division, was the first to enter Paris, at the head of his tanks, which he led all the way to the city hall, headquarters of the National Council of Resistance. This marked, in a way, the crowning of something started in French Africa four years earlier by a graduate of the school, Governor Félix Eboué, who on August 26, 1940, was the first to rally to

*The Fulani are a large African ethnic group (ed.).

General de Gaulle. ENFOM contributed to the triumph of Free France, and it went on training educated and brave men, capable of serving well overseas France.

Would anyone suggest that it would be better to forget these things because they belong to a colonial, even an imperial, past? Will someone maintain that the feelings the school's graduates expressed in letters they did not have to write—and in great acts they accomplished with complete abnegation at the time of France's occupation—have now been rendered meaningless by decolonization? We should listen to the head of state of an independent African country. Diori Hamani, president of Niger, while talking in 1970 to Rostain, a school graduate now the ambassador to Niger, emphasized "the moral and administrative teaching given by ENFOM," a school "where," he said, "I have had the privilege to teach and which produced so many administrators whose strength, good citizenship, and feeling for people can be used as models by our own leaders."

Sources

1. "L'Ecole coloniale," in *De Vorming van den bestuursambtenaar voor over-zeesche gewesten in Nederland, Engeland, Frankrijk, Belgie en Italie* (Leiden, 1937), pp. 100–107.
2. "Colo et chercheur," *Latitudes* (1963), pp. 5–9.
3. "L'Ecole peinte par ses élèves pendant les années sombres," in *Derniers chefs d'un empire*, ed. Pierre Gentil, Travaux et mémoires de l'académie des sciences d'outre-mer, n.s., no. 1 (Paris, 1972), pp. 17–20.

3

Colonial Policy

In much of his writings Delavignette surveyed the nature of French colonial policy, looking at its historic traditions, its contemporary developments, and its future prospects. Surveying the history of French colonialism from the Crusades to 1943, the time at which he was writing this article (1), Delavignette claimed that there had been a consistent commitment by France to the welfare of its overseas subjects. In the midst of the French debacle of World War II and the humiliating occupation by Germany, Delavignette upheld the image of a generous, self-sacrificing France whose glories had lain and could still lie in the colonies. Equally positive was the assessment of France's contribution to its colonies in the writings published on the occasion of the Paris International Colonial Exposition of 1931. In selections 2 and 3 he highlights French achievements by giving a rather negative account of precolonial Africa; the next essay (4) concentrates on the material contributions of French rule to Africa.

Of course there was room for improvements. In 1936 the left-wing Popular Front government came to power, and the new Socialist minister of colonies, Marius Moutet, attempted to introduce a series of overseas reforms. On the occasion of the thirtieth anniversary of the Popular Front, the Fondation nationale de sciences politiques held a conference to review that government's achievements. Delavignette was asked to consider Moutet's contributions in the colonial field. As Moutet's aide, Delavignette was intimately linked to policy-making, but he modestly refrained from spelling out the extent to which the minister's achievements were based upon his own counsel (5). On the whole Delavignette's assessment of Moutet's contribution was overly optimistic, for in the end Moutet's caution and the massive resistance from special-interest groups prevented many of the decrees from being carried out. But, of course, they remained important indicators of the will for reform.

Delavignette wrote a piece on retrospective views in 1939 of the French contribution to her empire. Rather somberly he drew up the balance sheet of French colonialism in the seventy years that the Third Republic had lasted after its founding in 1870. In this article he saw essentially a series of failures to close the gap between the promise and the reality of French imperialism, and he called on Frenchmen to commit themselves to their empire (6).

Although Delavignette was interested in the whole French empire, he knew only Africa, and it was to Africa that he returned again and again in his writings. France could fully understand its obligations to Africa, Delavignette thought, only if she could think of herself as forming a new unity with that continent, now the Eurafrican continent. In *Soudan-Paris-Bourgogne* he spoke for the first time of this link between the two continents (7). The necessity for closer bonds between France and Africa were further developed in the face of the German demand for a return of the colonies lost after World War I and given to France as mandate territories. In opposing this demand Delavignette fully articulated his thought on Eurafrica, claiming that the African territories were no longer colonies that could be bartered like merchandise. He affirmed that they had become part of France, forming with her an inseparable Eurafrican mass (8, 9). These ideas were later influential in setting the stage for the unitary empire that emerged after World War II, an empire in which all peoples were granted equal citizenship.

Economics had played an important role in the connection between France and her colonies. Although Delavignette had praised French contributions in health and food policies, he also understood that the overall picture was less than brilliant. In a scathing review in 1935 of French economic policies towards her colonies, Delavignette pointed out the failure of the French bourgeois to export his capital to Africa and of the government to develop the colonies socially and economically (10, 11). He warned that failure to make up for this neglect could lead to a rupture between the colonies and the motherland. It was common enough in the interwar years to discuss the need for economic development in the empire, but most of those advocating such policies tended to have an exploitative attitude toward the empire. One of the myths which developed during the Depression in France was that France's economic woes could be solved by sending unemployed Europeans as settlers to Africa. Delavignette strenuously opposed this policy. Europe needed to solve its economic policies at home before trying to spread its system abroad. Interestingly, Delavignette did not totally oppose white settlement in Africa, but he indicated that the time was not ripe (12).

One of the most important French economic projects in West Africa was the building of a vast irrigation system on the Niger River in French Sudan. Delavignette described the promise of the project but revealed what, for the era, was a sensitive appreciation for the human aspects of economic development (13, 14).

Delavignette reminded the French public that economic development, as all French goals in Africa, required a good knowledge of African societies, of the history, customs, and institutions of the colonial populations. In a passage in his *Afrique occidentale française*, he quickly sketched out the rich cultural legacy of West Africa (15). Knowledge of contemporary African society, Delavignette pointed out, was very difficult to acquire because of the prevalent European stereotypes and a lack of real interest in Africa. He attacked these attitudes savagely in a satirical passage in his first book, *Toum* (16). French rule could be more effective if the colonial administrator could overcome the gap separating him from the indigenous culture and thus gain control over a colonial situation which was in the process of change (17).

Once the indigenous culture and people were known, French rule could be fully effective only through the proper use of the already existing political authorities. French West Africa, with a population of 15 million, could not be ruled directly through a few hundred French administrators; the orders for tax collection, census-keeping, preserving order and customary justice were issued through local chiefs, regional and village. Delavignette understood the difficulties of the double role chiefs were asked to play: they were both representatives of their own people and agents of the French administration. Governor-General Brevié in the early 1930s attempted to strengthen the position of the chief by "modernizing" him, by giving him a Western education and an elected council which would presumably enlarge his popular support. Brevié thought that these reforms would prevent the chief from becoming a mere cog of the French administration, but in actuality they intensified the problem. Delavignette, in a series of articles, attempted to describe Brevié's policies, pointing out the extent to which the French had damaged the prestige and power of the chiefs and sapped them of real authority. Yet somehow Delavignette put his hope in Brevié's plans for modernization; it seemed the only way out of the dilemma (18). The power of the chiefs ought to be increased, Delavignette wrote, but the French could not allow them to lead their societies in a backward direction; the chiefs had to be supervised and educated so that they could help lead the evolution of their societies (19, 20).

Most of Africa was rural, and in that milieu the problems of French control and rule could be seen essentially as connected with the nature of African chiefdom. But in the urban centers a French-educated elite was emerging, taking on French values. These "new Africans" were often ridiculed by Frenchmen, but Delavignette was one of the few administrators to describe their development and take seriously their demands and aspirations. And, also exceptionally, Delavignette recognized that, even outside the urban centers, a "Frenchified" group was emerging in the bush, made up of veterans from the First World War who were no longer willing to live in the traditional manner—or to accept uncritically French rule. Delavignette urged the French government to understand these changes and meet the demands of the veterans (21).

Serving this "Frenchified" group, a small coterie of French-writing African journalists published a number of newspapers and magazines. While not totally devoid of some sense of bemusement, Delavignette's article in 1935 on the Dahomey press also includes a sensitive appreciation for the plight of these journalists caught between two cultures (22).

Commenting on the plays performed by the African students of the Ecole William Ponty of Gorée, Delavignette wrote of a successful fusion of African and French values. He saw their plays as symbolizing the benefits each culture could gain from the other. Thus, Delavignette argued, the French educational system did not necessarily have to uproot the African but rather could help him appreciate his own culture while at the same time giving him the tools to change it (23).

In the middle of the nineteenth century, when the French had had minor possessions in Senegal that contained only a few thousand Africans, they had extended to these Africans the rights of French citizenship; the people born in what later came to be known as the "four communes" (Gorée, Saint-Louis, Rufisque, and Dakar) were thus part of the French political system. As French conquest continued in the nineteenth century, these political rights were not extended, and the colonial administration saw the rights of the four communes increasingly as an anomaly, something preferably to be abolished. But Delavignette prophetically viewed the active participation by Senegalese citizens in the French political systems as a model for the rest of French-speaking Black Africa. He anticipated events by some fifteen years (24).

1   The Civilizing Mission
The French Colonial Tradition

Our colonial history reveals France's importance and calling in the world and the part she will play in Europe's future.

That history began during the Middle Ages, in Asia Minor with the Frankish kingdom in Jerusalem. It began again in the modern era, unfolding in North America and in the West Indies, in Southern India, and in the islands of the Indian Ocean. A continuous thread in this story is the long rivalry which opposes France to England, from 1685 to 1815, which momentarily ceased when the English took India and our American empire. The French empire reemerged in the nineteenth century, in 1830. It spread to the African continent, creating French Africa by settling us on both sides of the Mediterranean and joining Western Black Africa to North Africa. It is present in Madagascar and in the Far East where the Indochinese Union was formed.

During these three long time-spans, our colonial history is not a continuous curve but a broken one, with forward and backward movements, which at times seem to express individual heroic acts rather than a national effort.

Nevertheless this history has an underlying unity which draws all of France into it. This unity comes from the variety of France's actions, because evangelization, exploration, and civilization go hand in hand. Colonialism is not a marginal aspect of our history; on the contrary, it is an important *achievement*, tightly connected to both our domestic and foreign policies.

This history unfolds not only on continents but also on oceans, but navigation alone does not explain the development of the empire. A vast program of civilization does. On a world map our colonies do not appear as man-made objects but as living countries. They cannot be understood if their climates are ignored. French colonization integrated the colonies into a worldwide civilization without destroying the native civilizations. We had a double impact; one influence from France itself and the other that we encouraged from the depths of the African and Asian continents.

Our colonies are not disconnected parts of the mother country or the branches of a company whose headquarters are in Paris. The empire joins masses of people so they can build a civilization. They are bound to one another and to European France. They constitute an empire which tends to become a community inspired by social programs.

This empire is not set against Europe; this community is not located outside Europe. On the contrary, Europe cannot exist without France and without France's colonies. We do not, however, want to subordinate this empire to the mother country. And, indeed now we are witnessing the emergence of a community within which mother country and colonies will retain their own talents and have their own functions. Now a new policy is being formed, a policy which deals with the Asian and African masses and which is called the native policy. Thus, our colonial history reveals the French position in the world, and this is a position that concerns Europe and its relationship to other continents, as well as the problem of racial balance.

We need more and more flexibility in our colonial policy, for a black obviously is not an Asian and the native policy in Africa cannot be similar to that in Indochina. Furthermore, we should know that in the same federation of colonies the native population which seems homogeneous at first glance is, in reality, very diverse. In AOF, a Dahomean is not a Senegalese, and the difference between a black from the Coast and a Sudanese black is greater than that between a man from Marseilles and one from Flanders.

We should know too that natives change, that their customs and morals are not rigidly fixed and that they are prone to undergo quick and silent transformations. A worthwhile native policy should take this into account and never lose contact with the people; it should also guide without coercing or attempting to lead too quickly.

A native policy cannot be improvised. It cannot be carried out by muddling through. It must be based on knowledge and not on finding ways out of thorny situations; it proceeds from a searching, open mind and not from a bureaucratic attitude. It does not oscillate between authoritarianism and generosity; it is ruled by the facts of human geography and by the progress of the diverse social sciences. From the start, we did not separate colonization from civilization, and we tried to civilize our colonies not just by transplanting our ideas but by understanding the different countries and by befriending their populations.

2   The Civilizing Mission
The French Peace: I

A certain Africa is gone forever, an Africa which lived yesterday and which we can now contemplate as a separate entity.

There is an important port in Dakar, a roadstead in Conakry, wharves in Bassam and Cotonou, and I did not have to face the sandbar in a canoe. There are roads in Timbuctu, Gao, and Zinder, and I traveled more often by car than on camelback.

And between the sandbar and the desert, between the two shores now accessible, lies a new country made from a very old continent. One can feel a new order of things which combines life-giving currents, one from France and another from ancient Africa.

Railways, roads, telegraphs streak native paths. Colonial cities loom amidst black villages and immemorial lands.

Camel-drivers guiding their caravans did not threaten me with their spears nor did the Kroumen with their arrows. And I found within the faraway tiny posts, in the heart of Africa, a very deep feeling of peace and friendship.

According to Rabelais, Africa is inclined to "give birth to monsters." And Gobineau talked about the "magnificent fears lurking around the dark continents." And we, colonial administrators in Africa, we start by quoting statistics: a surface of 5 million square kilometers; a population of 13.5 million inhabitants; a railway system covering 3,200 kilometers, 46,000 kilometers of roads and 22,000 kilometers of telegraphic wires; exports and imports amounting to 13,000 tons and 2,775,000,000 francs.

The reader will obviously believe that I looked up these figures for my present purpose and that I was unfamiliar with them before describing the Africa I have come to know. He should question other colonial administrators. He will discover that they spontaneously and joyfully quote kilometers, tonnages, and millions of francs, if not for all of AOF at least for their own colony or district.

A certain harmony comes out of these figures. But, in order to be moved, one must realize how vast West Africa is and how scarce man, whether black or white, is; one must visualize the immense labor involved, must himself mark out the new road, himself count the money which flows coin after coin, note after note, in the new European store and in the native market where the white man shops for the first time.

This harmony also encompasses the residency with its mango-lined alley. At its extremity, I still catch a glimpse of a sinister serpent: the old Southern trail taken by slaves and their owners. But it is disappearing in the fields. There are no more slave traders. A factory is smoking, trucks are humming. They carry to the railway station vats filled with peanut oil which will be delivered 8,000 kilometers from here, in Marseilles.

Do I rejoice when I look at a factory, trucks, the intricate web of business and become aware that districts formerly engulfed by the Sudanese savannah are now becoming parts of the worldwide circulation of wealth? Yes, but there is also something else. There is the land. The factory, the road, and my residency itself owe their existence to the land, to the fields.

Between the sandbar and the desert a flag is present but also the soil of France—a land piously cultivated and inhabited. The French peace which reigns in Africa has given us the admirable habit of being united to strange and diverse men, and it fills us with a glorious and joyful mystery.

And it is this tie which joins all Africans together. While thunder is heard in the dark night, some natives and the white man tell stories about the French peace. "Before the French came, my father was a bandit," says the driver. And we all laugh. Bandits do not exist anymore. One of Samory's sons who was going to the Ivory Coast to claim his credit (meaning that he was trying to get reimbursed for a debt) remains silent not because he objects to such talk but out of dignity. The Moor horse dealer (should I confess that his magnificent head of hair frightens me!) who is driving a herd to the lower part of the coast remains silent also, but what kind of a trial would be his if he had to pay tolls from one Africa to another, give presents, be at the mercy of kinglets who would control "his route." And my host, a former infantryman, has taken out of his painted trunk a modest khaki jacket that he wears for special occasions. He gives it to me so I can warm up. I enjoy these refined attentions from humble people and I think that all men, from the distrustful Déda who still moves forward with noiseless tread in the forest, and who used to string his bow as soon as he saw another Déda, to the Senegalese voter who writes about public affairs in a Dakar newspaper, all the vast and varied African population are paying homage with us to this wondrous peace.

3 The Civilizing Mission
The French Peace: II

Let us try to reconstruct broadly the way things were when colonization and the great explorations began.

The Guinea and Ivory Coast forests, lakes, and swamps were hiding places for unruly populations who barely subsisted. Human sacrifices were performed in Dahomey. Senegalese fought among themselves. And let us just think about the recent times when Dahomeans and Senegalese did not know of one another's existence. Whether they were spread over vast areas or concentrated, the native societies were stagnating. It is true that they were experiencing some Islamization. But Ousman Dan Fodio in the east (Haussa country), and then El Hadj-Omar in the West (Toucouleur country) were conducting a bloody proselytism. Samory, who came afterward, was less a prophet than a warmonger, a gang leader.

In short, nowhere could a strong state be found. Of course, ancient civilizations had shone, especially in Sudan, although they were not known in Europe; but their inner force was gone, they did not shine anymore. Most of the time, one felt he was witnessing a miserable way of life, stuck away in some savannah, forest, or desert corner.

Great evils were at the root of Africa's squalor. Everywhere communications, crops, wealth, and human life were precarious—and this precariousness was not, after all, invented by colonial propaganda.

To unite all the different Africas, to join them with roads and railways, to dig ports, to secure peace and trade, to protect agriculture, to free slaves, to build schools and clinics, to establish the reign of justice—in a word, to erect a colony was our achievement.

4 The Civilizing Mission
The Clinic and the Granary

In order to recognize the good, we do not have to shout about evil and promise miracles. There are many evils in French West Africa. No miracles take place there, but good is being accomplished.

Here is the health balance-sheet for the past year: sources of yellow fever contagion have been spotted, the fight against leprosy has been organized for the first time, the prophylaxis against sleeping sickness has been applied, plague has been reduced in Senegal (no deaths from the plague in Dakar in 1931, and far fewer deaths in other areas) and a collective health plan has been set up there.

You may object that all this medical apparatus is not the solution to the crisis. You may want to discuss the present [economic] crisis, but remember, the black population should not feel left alone during these hard times. Can you give them money in exchange for their cocoa and peanuts? Very little? Then, if you cannot make them richer, at least help them get rid of plague and leprosy. Thus, they will know that you are still their leaders.

We will go to them and not wait for them to come to the clinic. Mobile health units and social workers will cover the whole country, eradicating centers of epidemics, and will constantly keep in touch with the bush population.

To work for mankind is to store up wealth for the future and feelings of loyalty for today. It is to act.

To work for mankind is, first of all, to save babies. We deplore the fact that we cannot multiply the number of visiting nurses who could help the midwives trained in Dakar. Those already on the job have been a great success, at Bouaké for example.

All things are related, and there cannot be a good health policy without a food policy. Reserve granaries to protect the growers against speculation in grains; mutual insurance cooperatives to encourage the blacks' natural tendency to act together and to allow them to use agricultural financing; rural schools with teachers in touch with experimental farms; women's education which will deeply influence family life; centers for native colonization which will spread all over the country;* all these remedies, some already carried out and others in the process of being implemented, converge toward the same ideal: to allow man to be man.

Not a man of theory but a man of action, Black Africa's homo faber.

French West Africa rests on a strong foundation: its peasants. Anything that would not be favorable to them would be deleterious;

---

*Delavignette saw the education of women as related to food policy since they would acquire information about nutrition. By "native colonization" he meant new settlements by Africans which would clear the land and establish newly cultivated areas (ed.).

anything built without them would be useless. This has been understood, and the masses' education is finally being dealt with.

5 The Civilizing Mission
Reforms of the Popular Front

Among all the ministers, the minister of the colonies had perhaps the most complex task because he had to be concerned with the world scene. He seemed to possess a lot of power, but in practice he had difficulty injecting a new spirit into the administration and making sure his orders were followed. These difficulties were due to the fact that he had to mobilize the European settlers and administrators as well as the masses, whose uniqueness and social structures were not clearly understood by the mother country.

Those, very briefly, were the conditions under which Marius Moutet began the colonial policy of the Popular Front; as soon as he became minister he defined both goals and means.

According to Léon Blum, it is important to "extract from the colonial system all the humanity it contains," to better the life of the colonial people by having them participate in the shaping of their own future. On June 24, 1936, Marius Moutet wrote: "A colonial system cannot survive unless it is operated from within by the natives who are supposed to benefit from it." He also said: "Colonies must not be organized around the mother country but with a view to forming with it an entity acceptable to all."

He made them understand that they should prepare the way for native participation in public affairs, evoking in the colonial administration itself as well as in the native elite a current of opinion open to rethinking colonial problems.

Measures for Social Improvement

Against famine. One of Moutet's first goals was an all-out effort against famine. On June 24, 1936, he asked that famine no longer be considered an acceptable natural event. He had a survey conducted as part of an ethnosociological research project so that his actions would be based on accurate information from the areas involved. On February 20, 1937, conclusions from that survey were incorporated in a socio-economic development plan which had already been put into practice in the field of workers' protection.

Workers' protection. From Indochina to Black Africa, a series of decrees abolished night work for women and children in factories, reduced the number of hours worked, and ruled that every worker was entitled to a yearly paid vacation. In Indochina, the Justin Godart mission was sent to stop the actions of the "slavers" who "exported" coolies. Factory inspection became a reality in French West Africa (AOF). Through the decree of July 13, 1937, the district of the Ivory Coast (Upper Volta) was created in order to prevent the Mossis peasants from being conscripted and sent to work on the southern timber sites. The June 17, 1937, law ratified the Geneva Convention of June 1930 and constituted a crucial text which abolished forced labor. It was made applicable to all the colonies through a decree on August 12, 1937.

Repression of usury. Equally important was the October 9, 1936, decree which, after an investigation ordered by a memorandum of August 11, 1936, suppressed usury in all the colonies. The evil of usury was one of the significant causes of forced labor, poverty, and under-nourishment.

The great program of small works in conjunction with important public works. The ministry launched the idea of a "great program of small works" on a village scale. There was the potential for local development in regions where agriculture was not developed but where there were valuable traditions that could form an economic foundation. Small modern agricultural implements could be adapted, and rural hydraulics could be furthered by the development of existing dams and wells. Thirty years later, Technical Cooperation [The French Peace Corps] was to make its own the concept of "basic agricultural investment." Marius Moutet saw his program of small works as coordinated with large public works such as ports, railways, roads, and airports. Thus, he decided to build the port of Abidjan and, after conducting his own investigation, had the Sansanding dam built.

The colonial fund. It would be impossible to promote the betterment of the masses if the colonies had to laboriously take from their own resources the funds necessary for their development. Moutet vigorously encouraged the colonial fund, which he saw as the way of using the solidarity of the mother country to give to the colonies a financial endowment which would enable them to purchase the basic elements of an infrastructure.

Measures towards Political Emancipation

*Dismantling of the "Indigénat."** The indigenat was a kind of disciplinary code, used unilaterally by the administrative power. It was dismantled everywhere through a series of exemptions.

*The *indigénat* code gave French administrators the right to sentence colonial subjects to a fine of up to 100 francs or fifteen days of jail, without trial or other form of due process, for infractions which were rather loosely defined (ed.).

Amnesty law. Indochinese political prisoners were freed.

Councils of leading citizens. Such councils, already functioning in French West Africa, were encouraged by Moutet and given greater authority. They served as a model for French Equatorial Africa, where in 1942 Félix Eboué was to emphasize them for his native policy. He wrote continuously and lectured the governors on the need to loosen the old chains of authoritarian rule.

Through his persuasive personality and the authority of the ministry, which made these reforms politically irreversible, Marius Moutet made a contribution that, in other forms, under other names, is the inspiration for the studies currently being carried out by the industrial nations in cooperation with and for the development of the Third World. Priority for that which is human, the betterment of the human condition for all peoples—for him these phrases were not empty rhetoric to be spoken and then forgotten as one turned to everyday affairs.

Historians will view all of his achievements as laying the foundation of the political emancipation of overseas peoples in conjunction with their economic, social, and cultural development.

6 The Civilizing Mission
Colonies in the Third Republic

As long as geographical explorations and military expeditions were carried out, the mother country kept abreast of events in the colonies; she was understanding of the new continents that were opening up. These events were interesting to read about when they were accompanied by martial drawings in the illustrated portion of the people's *Petit Journal* or when they were permeated with a proper kind of exoticism in the bourgeois *Le Tour du Monde*. But when social responsibility had to be assumed for hundreds of thousands and tens of millions of men and when bonds of unity had to be forged, the mother country pretended no longer to understand. What! Were not victories and exploration of new regions enough in themselves? Scandals which broke out in these colonies irritated the mother country.

The Republic would have liked to give the natives a representative to defend their interests in Paris. But such proposals were aborted with the realization that the natives were illiterate and unable to exercise their vote freely or that they had no inclination for parliamentary institutions. The only solution was an active, powerful administration, motivated by humanism. But this kind of administration is not found in textbooks or in the everyday notions of our civilized way of life.

The 1914 war was set in motion by German imperialism. As a consequence, colonial questions gained a new importance.

The colonies sent 700,000 infantrymen and workers as well as 5 million tons of merchandise! France was thus represented everywhere in the world, in Africa and Asia, in the South Seas and in the Indian Ocean, and that presence was embodied by men of all colors. The colonies gave the mother country soldiers and sacrificed themselves for her sake. In France they no longer aroused exotic curiosity when attending an exposition or a Fourteenth of July parade. They came as human beings ready to fight for the survival of free men. This was the first instance of its kind in history. Although a few could already notice the emergence of a worldwide French community, many did not understand that a revolution was under way. Worn out by her victory, France was clinging to the concept of colonies as possessions. It was as if she had forgotten that, after all, there was more to the foundation and development of colonies than career opportunities, a thirst for adventure, a desire to enlarge present possessions and spread around a certain material progress. At the root of colonization are also great moral motivations: evangelization, an antislavery policy, a thirst for knowledge, and a love of freedom.

Economically, the mother country could not or did not know how to give the colonies the help they expected. Before the war, France had invested its money abroad (one-third of its 113 billion francs in gold). Now, it was faced by the task of rebuilding twenty departments, with reimbursing very large debts. Nevertheless, it allowed banks to speculate on foreign currencies and its people to dabble in colonial firms.

As far as Asia and Africa were concerned, she did not go further than to continue traditional prejudices which stated that the Vietnamese were inscrutable and the Senegalese were overgrown children. The colonial administrators continued in their routine, all the while noticing that the "inscrutable" Vietnamese and the "childish" Senegalese had eyes to measure the battlefield of a future struggle.

The mother country was suffering an economic crisis. Germany, just next door, was rearming. Europe was searching for peace and prosperity in Africa, for an end to unemployment by the development of the black continent. Africa became Europe's work site and its salvation. These themes were often heard in the mother country. Was international cooperation going to be organized? No, the problem was to redistribute territories and populations among competitive imperialist powers. Ten years after a victory gained in part by black men, the necessity of "redistributing" the colonies was discussed. Were these colonies still just possessions where natives did not belong to themselves?

France has other relationships with its overseas territories than just those based on power. There is a French colonization which goes beyond a mediocre colonial particularism: it is the opposite of racism and it

invites men of all races to enjoy political and civil liberties, to stand free
before the law and be brothers. Why, then, does it seem now to lack the
necessary energy to go on?

The regime has lost its feeling for its people as well as for the enemies
of its people. The old Bourbon monarchy under the Restoration crum-
bled because of its extremists. The Third Republic has no extreme
supporters, only indifferent ones. It has ministers, civil servants, soldiers,
and militants, who more often than not are "quasi-republicans."

But despite all this, the republican promise of the French people still
shines brightly on the overseas territories.

7   Eurafrica
A New Province

I have served in Sudan, worked in Paris, and lived in Burgundy. Thus
three lands roam in my mind; three countries, all worthy of a man.

While looking at the map and thinking about my three households, I
discover that Sudan, despite its strangeness, its still exotic makeup, is
now part of the Western world, as well as Paris and this Burgundy which
formerly was the seat of a great Western duchy.

From the far end of the Sudanese bush, I realize I am traveling towards
a new West.

8   Eurafrica
The German Challenge: I

You talk of giving back to Germany its former colonies. This is the
language of the past. The mother country is no longer the sole owner
who can sell or give back a possession. The colony can no longer be
defined as the Encyclopedists defined it: "made by and for the mother
country." Obviously, you cannot have a colony without a mother
country, neither can you have it without natives who cooperate. The
colony of today belongs as much to the native country as to the mother
country. Will you ignore the warning issued by the emerging new world?
If you do, you will be carrying on the policy of old, unable to insure
peace.

A change is in order. The British, Belgians, Portuguese, and French
should cooperate in a common West African plan to establish a program
of large public works and small-scale rural infrastructures, a customs
union, a money and credit system, and an intercolonial legal system.
These things are now easier to achieve since the nations already agree on
certain agrarian policies. This can be done today: organize an African
cooperation with native and European elements which have already
proven themselves ready for it.

Cooperation leads us to a new Eurafrican world, but it will be fruitful only if we play an active role in this cooperation and if we are strong internally. This idea will be difficult for the public to accept. The simplistic notion of "restitution" appears to be an easy solution. But restitution to Germany of its former colonies with or without compensation, with or without a complete reexamination of territorial allotments, is not really a solution. It does not entice us to work for peace; it would be a loss for Europe.

There can be no colony or mandate without the continued development of the natives. And equally there can be no colony or mandate without a mother country that will reform itself. Let us face racist and totalitarian states with a counterreform. Let us not see in our African heritage a source of a life annuity that would allow us to go on in a cowardly way with our present life-style. Colonies are not the easy way out. In fact, they embody Pascal's notion of duty: "We thus have to combine justice and power in order to accomplish this. We have to succeed in making powerful what is right and in making right what is powerful."

Once this is done it will be possible to create a strong, new institution capable of facing up to German activities. A Eurafrican bloc will be born, and this bloc will check Germany's pressure.

Can Germany have a part in this? If she is not one power against four others but one among five, she will accept the practical conditions of working in common. Racism then will seem less urgent an issue than organizing agricultural production, mineral prospecting, trade networks, sanitary commissions and solving concrete problems while taking into account the four other members of the team.

Meanwhile, let us start at the beginning. Let us establish the team which Germany will want to join.

And let us remember that the Eurafrican team does not preclude our being strong; on the contrary it will show whether or not we possess strength and vitality.

9 Eurafrica
The German Challenge: II

Germany craves African colonies in the old meaning of the word, but she is aware that soon they will no longer exist. She uses the language of the past—colonies—when speaking to the diplomats, but she uses a different one when speaking to her people: that of the African future. She takes African countries down from their old frames where they still hang as genre pictures on chancellery walls, away from masses and propaganda. Germany knows that the old diplomatic hierarchy among continents does not exist any more and that Black Africa is a square in the European chess-board. She knows that tomorrow there will be no Europe or Africa, only a Eurafrican world. No longer will we find colonies in Africa and mother countries in Europe; there will be Eurafrican empires, which is a very different matter. And the Reich with its Deutsche Mittelafrika wants to be the first to participate in this new world. The concepts of colony and mother countries are merging in the new concept of empire; Africa and Europe are fusing into a different world, which will extend from snow-covered forests to cotton fields (the way the U.S.A. extends from Maine to Louisiana), and Germany wants to occupy its middle region.

By opposing Deutsche Mittelafrika and the return of Togo and the Cameroons to Germany, we are not acting as radical colonialists or as representatives of a group indifferent to peace in Europe and blind to the Eurafrican evolution. On the contrary, it is because we want this Eurafrican evolution to lead to peace in Europe that we cry "Beware!" to those who believe they are giving back "colonies" in the old sense of the word while in fact they will help build a German empire stretching from middle Europe to middle Africa.

Africa must be included in the common task; we must elaborate institutions in agreement with the native populations. French administrators, by carrying out in the Cameroons the same rural and native policy as in AOF, by organizing not a paganistic cult of the soil but the work of black peasants, have already contributed to the making of this new Eurafrican world.

10   Economic Policies
The Nineteenth-Century French Bourgeois and the Colonies

If we examine the relationship of the French bourgeois to the black colonies, we discover a paradoxical mixture of generosity and avarice.

He is undoubtedly generous, with words and even with political deeds. Because of the philosophic influences of the eighteenth century and the French bourgeoisie's very old Christian belief, blacks are treated as men and considered part of mankind. These humanistic and religious traditions honor the bourgeoisie.

However, this generosity is in practice fouled by a vile avarice. It is believed that colonies do not have to be endowed: they are like daughters born out of wedlock who would legally and scandalously be recognized if given dowries. All they need are very modest pensions.

Are we writing antibourgeois literature? Let us talk figures. Out of a fortune evaluated before the war at 113 billions francs (in gold), bourgeois France—so prudent!—invested or rather risked 40 billion abroad. She could loan only 6 billion to all her colonies. And how much to those in Black Africa? In AOF, for example, about 200 million, and for the most part just before the war.

Thus the time has come for a new and significant reform. It is on colonial matters that the bourgeois will have to apply perhaps his finest quality, his passion for working for justice and freedom.

But if the bourgeois lacks audacity, if he confines himself to colonial stinginess, if he does not dare take the lead in a new humanism, these colonies which could be his salvation will then cause his downfall. He will lose them, or rather they will destroy him.

11   Economic Policies
Neglect

France is not very concerned about AOF, except to preach thrift, a virtue she does not practice herself. We build racetracks for cars in Paris while Sudanese roads have only primitive bridges. Stables in the French provinces are electrified while no good wells are available to the Senegalese people. We may send them an engineer, who will cost them 100,000 francs a year, to design a new railroad system, but along the already existing one a village will not be able to afford the 300 francs necessary to cement a well to be dug by the villagers. In France, there is a surplus of unused capital. Africa, where lie the new riches, will vegetate because Frenchmen are either paralyzed by the desire to save money or carried away while pursuing an illusion.

12   Economic Policies
The False Lure

Unemployment is an evil that is another form of slavery. But can we believe that giving African lands or herds to our unemployed will solve the problem? I am writing this article in a small French town situated in a deserted rural region overlooking run-down villages and fields that lie fallow.

And while we think of sending Frenchmen to replace native herdsmen in the Sudanese savannah, our own country's sheep farms are unable to recruit shepherds; and while we dream about pioneers who will clear swampy forests, we have to send for Spanish woodcutters to work in our own forests.

Indeed we know why Africa seems more attractive as a place to work: the lure is empty space, freedom, power, and exoticism. It softly says, "You will be a ruler in Africa."

It is still in European France that we can most easily create riches. It is there, however, that to redistribute them is the most difficult, but is this a sufficient reason to avoid this very serious problem? Do we believe we can solve the problem by sending our unemployed to AOF or AEF, where riches are meager?

No task is impossible for our machines. One day, they will make the tropical and the equatorial zones suitable for the European farmer. Let it be! But we should start at the beginning: European France first of all should reorganize its own economy; only by doing this will it remain an active and influential mother country.

13   Economic Policies
The Dam

I begin by reminiscing about the last thirty years in Sudan. How things happened in one generation! The fight against those who advocated slavery; social unrest brought about by the abolition of slavery; recruitment for the French war after the 1913 famine; "prosperity," that is to say, construction of 30,000 kilometers of road through forced labor and "increased" production, which required going from the family unit to a larger one in order to enter world trade; monetary crisis, as a result of abruptly falling commodity stocks and rising prices for manufactured products, a double tragedy for the native, who accused us of betraying his people. In thirty years, how many shocks! It is high time we took care of the land which suffered all this and made the Sudanese land fertile through Stin [Nigerian Irrigation Service].

The Sudan has survived African wars, slavery, [problems caused by] the freeing of rural slaves, famines, infantry recruitment, and the urgent demands of trade. It now suffers the brunt of the Depression. Stin will save it. But an insidious question haunts me: what if Stin fails? What if, instead of saving, it burdens the Sudan even more?

Stin is a world in itself with working sites, a bureaucracy, and ideas about Sudan and the natives. Stin wants, if not to assimilate the Niger River to the Nile River, whose fertilizing floods are more important than the Niger's, at least to make agricultural land from a dry region of half a million hectares* with the help of dams and canals.

Stin's plans are as grandiose as its means. Great plans are elaborated for the small region of Baguinda, and on the site of Segou-Senegal there will be more and more peanut cultivation. On the Ivory Coast there will be cocoa and coffee. In addition AOF needs a region where agriculture is strong; where grains, herds, and labor are plentiful. The region of the Niger bend, transformed by irrigation, will be such a center. There, where the population reaches one hundred inhabitants per square kilometer, a density unknown before in Africa, doctors, schoolteachers,

*A hectare is approximately 2.5 acres (ed.).

and administrators will find successful conditions for their work. Not only will this irrigated region be very useful to the Coast, it will be indispensable to the [planned] Trans-Saharan railway. If it does not prosper, the train running through the desert will smash into a land of great poverty. The waters of the great river will contain, in the canals installed in the fields, the vital element that will shape the future of AOF. And from the Atlantic coast to the Mediterranean, a new African world will flourish; its strong foundation will lie on the Niger.

Why am I skeptical about such a plan? Could it be that to me Sudan is not some "productivity" to be increased but a country which has a right to live as it chooses? In case, wherever it was possible, the natives themselves have started rice cultivation. Why not develop and improve on what they have done, instead of concentrating all means on one region alone?

For at least two centuries blacks were brought as slaves to the West Indies and to America in order to furnish us with sugar, coffee, and cotton. Will we, with the help of technological progress, enslave them again, and this time in their own countries?

I hope that Stin will succeed in irrigating half a million hectares but without burdening or uprooting the existing villages. I hope that the Nigerian Office will populate its new, fertile land and that it will succeed—but with the help of free peasants!

14   Economic Policies
Some Shadows

We are talking about important public works in Africa. I do not say that they should not be realized, but something disquiets me. I want to warn against two dangers.

The first one is the tendency to excess inherent in industrialization. It gives birth to economic gods which awe and frighten men. When we say "important public works," we utter words which tend to encompass the whole colonial activity and accomplishment. Important public works! They justify everything! Porterage as well as the transferring of native populations and the breaking up of families. We are already witnessing an Africa dominated not by administrators but by engineers. In order to protect Africa from America will we "Americanize" Africa?

Because these works will require natives to be organized in worker-camps, we one day will be dealing with a militant proletariat. The black peasants of Africa will no longer exist, and I cannot imagine what Europe will have gained from it.

The other day I heard people talk about an African railway system which crosses a desert region. "We will populate it!" they said. "We will lure alongside the railway tribes which stubbornly keep on leading miserable lives in the faraway bush." I am not sure this is right. The railway may indeed lure people. We know of some instances in which this has happened. It may also keep the desert the way it is. We also have examples of that. To first install "the important public works" and then be concerned with the men is, I am afraid, the course of action offered to Africa by European industrialization.

The second danger lies in the fact that Africa is not very well known. In the above case, we want to impose the railway system on the country, and if the country remains a desert we will not acknowledge that this is the fault of our planning. Is this hubris? Not really, but it is determination without a knowledge of Africa. We already have made too many mistakes because we wanted to "develop" African countries after a cursory look at them, without any serious attempt to study them.

15   Knowing the Natives
Africa and its History

Natives and colonials appear to one another as mysterious beings.

Being single, we do not understand families, women, and children who live in the native community. Having lived on books, we do not relate to men anymore and they look to us very different from ourselves. As city dwellers, we see savages in peasants; their culture and their intelligence remain impervious to our understanding. We forget that they see in nature symbols that we can no longer recognize, that have meaning now lost to us.

Religion and friendship make them feel very close to animals. In my last residency, Gouin peasants worshipped the boa as guardian of their fields and the Senofos revered the crocodile as a bridge-builder in the rice plantations. These superstitions were at first tools with which to explore the world; today they remain as justifications of a life which we reject. We would have to bring back our primeval soul in order to feel at ease with native customs and to live in communion with Africa.

We have to decipher yet another mystery, which springs from the difference existing between the dreams of our colonization and our first results. Maybe this difference is nothing more than a delay since we think faster than we act; our minds cannot comprehend everything. But it appears that natives are no longer what they used to be and that they have not become what we would have liked them to become. It is as if the colony suggests but some unknown God decides. This is why we now have to remain sensitive and search painstakingly and devotedly for the truth which unites us to the Africans, to correct mistakes and go on building French West Africa.

We often call Africans big children. But it is we who are childish when we think they did not exist before us and created nothing.

Curse the colonial who has no appreciation for the native past. He does not understand the country he lives in and performs badly.

AOF is made up of very old countries with their own traditions and chronicles, countries that knew, much before the French themselves, important events, great men, emperors, prophets, wise men, revolutions, wars. It is obviously difficult to write of this portion of history. There are no archives, no stone monuments, no medals. The desert windstorms and the winter rains have destroyed all things of the past, and man, alone and wild, seems to be born every year as if the world had just begun.

The African land does not retain the natives' traces, and who knows what it will keep of the colonial domination! We thus have only word-of-mouth tales and, from traveling Arabs, a few notes such as the Ibn Batuta manuscript (1352–53). And when we think that in France, where documents and scholars abound, history remains a complex and lively entity which eludes the best history books, we realize how mysterious is the African past.

16   Knowing the Natives
An African Satire

The women are talking away and the men wait anxiously for their words as dogs wait for a bone.

The redheaded one, lisping:

"How nice it is here! I would love to live close to nature! The natives are gentle, aren't they?"

The captain, brushing his mustache, says:

"The population's attitude is good. Right now I am touring the colony and tracking down the rebellious ones. I do not think there are any here, but one should keep an eye on pilgrims and travelers."

Then, the commandant:

"I can vouch for the region I command. Natives pay their taxes diligently and accept forced labor gracefully."

The governor speaks up; melodious sentences flow out of a mouth fringed with tough hair:

"Civilization! Civilization! We are bringing these backward tribes forward into the modern economic world! We are injecting positivist science in large doses into these superstitious primitive populations!

We are molding the future face of mankind with the clay from these frozen societies!"

The captain cries:

"Let us recruit, let us recruit! Infantry, artillery, cavalry. Long live France!"

And the ladies coo:

"Let us take pictures, let us take pictures! Unusual country, traditional costumes. Ah! My dear, how exciting!"

"The governor does not realize how serious our difficulties are. He wants his road. And why, to travel it once a year in his car! Ah, but I will let him know!"

The other day, when the commandant was ordered to supply one hundred volunteers for the Damagaram battalion, he was crying:

"Disgusting! The people will flee into British Nigeria. The governor has never set foot in the bush country. One hundred volunteers! But this means that taxes are in jeopardy and maybe riots! Ah! I will warn him!"

The governor is here, dear commandant. But the commandant says "Yes, yes" to whatever the governor tells him. In the same way, all our chiefs say "Yes, yes" to whatever the commandant says.

The people in the administration know nothing but lies. The village chief lies to the sultan who lies to the commandant who lies to the governor who lies to I don't know whom but surely to someone.

And the white chiefs are very refined when it comes to lying. They lie to themselves. Deep down, they know that being soldiers in their armies, opening gates for their cars, exhausts and annoys us. But they say to themselves: "Poor people! It is for their own good! Civilization! Civilization!"

And the ladies are taking pictures.

"Ah!" says one of them who is educated, "these festivities, these fights, these tournaments, these singers, what a marvelous, medieval spectacle. My dear commandant, you are like a feudal lord among your vassals and serfs!"

"Good God, yes," says he approvingly, "it is not possible to understand these people if we forget that they have not evolved since the Middle Ages."

If you insist, commandant, if you insist! We do not have an idea of what these famous Middle Ages were. Maybe you will be frightened if you learned that we are timeless.

White men do not know what to do with us. We give them no books, no stones which would allow them to explore our past. They are baffled by our customs and they look in their memories for some remote traditions which would explain ours. They can see us as men only if they cover our faces with their ancestors' masks.

Whatever you do, dear white men, you will never understand us. Yet we are men capable of hatred and love.

17   Knowing the Natives
The Administrator's Duties

For a long time, native customs were considered oddities which did not interest serious-minded people. The intellectual, aesthetic, and ethical lives of the colonized populations were neither valued nor studied by the scientists but were known by the colonial administrators. Public opinion was fed by the idea that natives were primitive, backward, inferior, these three adjectives being the pedantic synonyms for the earlier term "savage."

But this is changing. Present research is starting to influence public opinion. We can no longer maintain these hierarchic divisions between the civilization of colonial peoples and ourselves. We realize that natives are not inferior human beings but different ones. They are being studied not to show their inferiority but their differences. We want to see them as they are, as men. We know that they are complex and natural and that, if we want to understand their complexities, we should not isolate them from their milieu, their epoch, or their way of life.

The colonial administrator is well aware that the native exists, that he is diverse, and that he is evolving. We find in the same colony native attitudes which are different from one another, which vary according to the geography and the race. We also find the attitudes of colonial natives shaped by a new milieu—the colony. This attitude stems from an amalgam of old and new values. Thus the colony, at first just an administrative construct and a hodgepodge of territories, is becoming a reality filled with life, a new fatherland for the natives.

[However, more research is needed.] No center for study and research exists, and, although the researchers do not get discouraged, they feel deeply the lack of such a center. Furthermore, the colonial administrators who in the past had decided that such research was their goal, and to whom it meant more, no longer head or initiate it. They no longer have the time or the means. Whereas the missionaries, for example, continually improve their knowledge of the natives, the administrators use data which are not up-to-date. They serve as hosts to well-meaning passersby who make "discoveries" about the colony and the natives that are already common knowledge.

Thus the natives evolve more rapidly than the administrators and the administration and in ways which the administrators, who remain confined to their official posts, ignore. It follows that there is an important gap between what the natives do and what we expect of them.

To remedy this situation we dream of an administrator who, instead of writing reports, would devote most of his time to observing his district, would enter his observations in the district diary and keep a file on the villages. A copy would be made each month and sent to the colonial capital, which would then have a better picture of the natives and their lives than the one contained in reports. The village file would serve as a kind of census where births, marriages, and deaths would be recorded, where local customs and their evolution would be noted.

Native policy [the sensitivity to native conditions and needs], which many colonies in the past seemed to discard in favor of worship of commercial production, today is making a comeback.

Especially at a time when natives are changing customs, destroying their former societies and their traditional chiefs, evolving in the direction of individualism, it is imperative that we again get in touch with them, follow them as men and help them to know themselves better.

18   Native Rule
Chiefs

The native chief is, above all, a man who has power and his power is two-sided: he represents his people and he has the investiture of our administration.

First of all, the chief must incarnate not only his ethnic milieu but also the province, the country, and the village he comes from. According to local custom, he either inherits his title or is elected. As Governor-General Brevié declared, "To follow customs when they are acceptable is still the best way to rule."

The chief, being from the region, has the trust of the region, and he should also have our trust. When dealing with the chiefs, we deal with natives whom we should understand and sympathize with; we should not take them for lowly civil servants.

Their education is very important. We need specialized schools and training programs where they will learn, among other things, that county chiefs should never dip into the tax funds.

M. Brevié does not want the chiefs to be treated as sergeant-majors, one interchangeable with the other, nor does he want them to behave like feudal lords. To insure their good behavior he has surrounded them with councils of notables.

These councils already exist at the village level: they are the elders' councils. The time has now come to use them. They act as a buffer between the administrative power and the natives. They scrutinize, nurse, and enlighten the masses. In order to function, Africa cannot be either harshly feudal or rigidly bureaucratic.

These councils of notables will lead, I believe, to the formation of a native nobility in the administrative corps. And it will be beneficial if, thanks to the village councils, these people remain in direct contact with rural families and the African soil.

At the political as well as the economic level, we are witnessing in this period of crisis a phenomenon of self-defense which, if I may, I will call "the africanization" of the colony. And this is a sign that the colony will endure and progress.

Far from diminishing the colonial administrators' role and activity, "africanization," on the contrary, requires powerful and outstanding civil servants.

19 Native Rule
A New Man—The Native Chief

For the colonial administrator, a chief is either a village chief, a canton chief, or a province chief. And this aptly describes his concept of what native power is: native power is a bureaucratic hierarchy, not a harmonious system of authentic values. Chiefs were like trees growing in a mystery-filled world, and he has turned them into wooden poles which he uses to enclose native affairs in an orderly garden drawn according to regulations. Chiefs enjoyed a power of religious origin and, by some strange absorption, this power supposedly passed into the colonial master's soul. The French commandant is tempted to believe that he is a master by divine right and that the native chiefs are nothing but employees.

We have already transformed the native chiefs into sergeant-majors who are very good at taking orders. Economically we are transforming them into nouveaux riches, in a society in which wealth and its use have radically changed. They are no longer the ancestral leaders people used to follow blindly.

We have now tried for a few years to give power back to the chief. The success of this change depends on the spirit that inspires it. This spirit could be dangerous if it is a conservative one. We should not hold on to a native feudal system which would be nothing more than a front. We should not exhume dead values. I believe that only nomadic chiefs have remained unchanged, unlike the sedentary ones who are becoming economic bosses. This is where we should exercise supervision. We should again listen to M. Brevié when he advocates education rather than eradication. However, we should not expect the chiefs to become perfect overnight. We should educate them so they do become worthy leaders.

20 Native Rule
Black Chiefs

As French West Africa was becoming organized, it was losing its native chiefs. Those who had not been broken by the military conquest had rapidly been worn out by the civil administration which required them to be obeyed as chiefs and to obey as clerks. Many of them disappeared under this regime. They were dependent on the personal and contradictory judgment of the successive commandants who expected, everywhere and every time, to find chiefs who were like themselves.

At the same time, roads, cities, and trade were creating new mores. The native milieu was getting harder and harder to know and rule. It, too, was breaking down its chiefs, and for a moment one could fear that French West Africa, hardly established, was already crumbling into scattered patches. Of course, local leaders had to be uprooted, if only to eradicate slavery and assert the power of the guardian country. But then, how could power be exercised? We could not persist long in believing that we could rule without chiefs, and we did not persist in it. But it took us longer to realize that to substitute one chief for another was not enough and that we should train some of them. It is never too late to act wisely. Traditional chiefs were still there or, if not they, their sons were. We very opportunely changed our policy toward them and this change bears fruit today. They now are respected. We are implementing a policy based on consideration for them, but consideration alone cannot make them what they should be: French West Africa's men of action.

In some places, it seems that people have, through material progress and economic development, acquired a taste for independence and that they do not care about having traditional chiefs anymore. While we go back to the chiefs, the people withdraw from them. Are we on the wrong track? By retaining the chief system, would we lose the populations? This indeed will happen if we do not educate the chief so he can be a leader of the masses. A policy based on consideration does not mean going back to the "good old days" or stopping a necessary evolution. Blacks tend naturally to go back to the primitive family system; if we allow their desire for freedom to be fulfilled, we are taking the risk of falling back into ancient Africa, which was narrow-minded, superstitious, closed, and divided into small, hostile clans.

To form chiefs who will become an active minority that will lead the evolution of French West Africa—that is now the aim of the program.

21 The New African
The Veterans

One complaint often voiced by civil administrators is that the former infantrymen lack social discipline. That's not surprising. Here is a Moaga, a Djerma, a Bambara, an African peasant. We remove him from his natural surroundings; we impose on him a new concept of himself while he is in the army. Then we would callously reassign him to his former position and expect him to have no reaction to it.

He has been used to regular paychecks, medical care, and abundant meals. He has been used to having a chief next to him who is present and accessible. Would he be human (and what barbarian trait would he not show?) if he accepted coldly the inequality embedded in native customs, the precariousness of rural life, and bureaucratic absenteeism?

We have made him more acutely aware of his first condition: he now feels its inadequacies. If he complains, he is thought to be anarchic and lazy. Most often, he becomes a canton chief's man in order to avoid being again a porter, an unskilled worker, or a forced laborer. It is then that he becomes bitter and joins in the conspiracies which surround our offices.

If we deal with him the way a sergeant-major would, we are not solving the problem we created by recruiting infantrymen. The former rifleman forces us to do what is right. And once again, so much the better. The more difficulties he creates for us, the deeper our common roots will become in the continent.

Anyway, all he asks for are "good things": land and a woman. And his woman has to be black. The legends which show him in some French barracks haunted by white women die hard, but all this time he has been longing for a black woman. While he is in the service, he saves enough money to pay for the dowry. From France, Morocco, or Syria, he can compete with the wealthy old men of his village. High wages and military bonuses thus promote proper unions and French "militarism" develops in young Africans a sense of individualism. The infantryman's money order may be the strongest force in AOF.

22   The New African
The Dahomey Press

The newspapers of Dahomey, despite their restricted circulation, are very important for our information. They substitute spontaneous testimonies for our own inquiry and awkward translations. And however awkward he may be in using French, the Dahomean journalist directly conveys to us his reactions stemming from his own sensitivity.

Let us open these newspapers. Let us glance at them, from the *Courrier du Golfe de Bénin* to the *Eveil-Togo-Dahomeén*; let us follow the *Phare*, the *Etoile*, the *Voix du Dahomey*; let us go from the *Presse Porto-Novienne* to the less important newspaper called *Vers la suprème sagesse*.

Their first characteristic is that they are written in an administrative style stuffed with familiar phrases. And the mixture is delightful.

In Black Africa, bureaucracy is like a queen whom her subjects imitate and whose language she often corrupts. She spreads pompous euphemisms. A village becomes a "community," the city an "urban center," goats "caprinae," the country chief "a dynast," and rain "an atmospheric precipitation." Everyone knows that colonization is the "planet's methodic exploitation," that a good colonial administrator's career is the "art of pulling together the conditions necessary to be assigned to a certain post or to solicit a promotion." The bureaucratic influence is such that it even invades trade! A shopkeeper whose business is doing badly exclaims, "I am overextended," and a fiancé who is in debt sighs, "In the red! I am in the red!"

I obviously haven't told everything about the Dahomean newspapers, but surely I have said enough to show their distinctiveness. Yet even when they unconsciously copy the mother country, they convey some aspect of their own land to us. And without them, we would know very little about the profound changes which are taking place there.

I would be very sorry if my Dahomean colleagues detected a deliberate criticism and an unfavorable attitude in my article. They should be praised for writing in French; I would be helpless if I had to write an article in Yoruba. But being deserving is not all, and I consider them too highly to only flatter them and not give them objective criticism.

I have the impression that the Dahomean writers are curious and intelligent, proud and somewhat skittish, readily trusting as soon as they are smiled at and even more readily drawn inward if they think they are being mocked; they worry that they might not be appreciated, or rather not be understood. Being men of experience in their own country and at the same time students anxious to attain European standards, they are their own harshest critics.

I have a great compliment and a great hope for them. I compliment them for doing their journalists' job, which is to provide and spread information. And I hope they will help us develop our French language in Black Africa. French is a treasure which is theirs as well as ours. Let them use it! These Dahomean journalists thus serve in their country the cause of French Africa.

23 The New African
*The Gorée Theater and
Franco-African Culture*

On August 12 and 17, on the stage of the Comédie des Champs Elysées, Paris became acquainted with the black theater of West Africa thanks to a company of student-teachers from the Gorée Normal School. Authors as well as actors, they created in French plays based on African themes. For two years they performed in Dakar and then had an opportunity to come to Paris. We realize that we are witnessing a landmark in the theater. This performance has ceased to be local entertainment and has taken its place in the world of theater; it is not a colonial phenomenon in the superficial meaning of the word, it is a landmark in our African history and reveals the success of a great and penetrating colonization.

This company of student-teachers makes us feel the authentic charm and the true expression of their African world. It is not exoticism for us anymore nor is it European imitation for them. Through dances and choruses, music and literature, a theater is being born which comes from their country and ours, from our language and theirs.

The young people who write the plays they interpret are neither artists nor authors. They want only to be schoolteachers. Coming from all parts of AOF and of different races, they know that the competitive examinations have gathered them for a while in the Gorée Normal School but that later on they will be scattered throughout West Africa. They are aware that they will teach in cities still in embryo, and without a theater in villages. They realize they will spend their lives among farmers. The theater they perform in Gorée is not outside the rural life they will share. It is impregnated with it; it proceeds from it and it will help them as rural schoolteachers. It has its roots in the soil and it will teach them to feel an Africa which, though developing, remains essentially agricultural.

The Gorée student-teachers possess the secret of primitive theater. But we would be mistaken if we thought they just unearthed old plays. These plays have changed with time.

The art of the primitive African theater has grown with elements taken from the colony and a new African world. The railway engine spitting out sparks is joined with the traditional animals found in folklore. The young people from Gorée were born in this new world which has assimilated our own inventions. They go back to their mother tongue, which contains the themes they use for creation, but they express in French what these themes suggest to them. It is more than a double translation. It is a new creation stemming from a grafted culture.

And this creation is an undeniable sign of a successful colonization. The Gorée Theater is a product of the method and spirit that characterize French colonization in West Africa.

24   The New African
The Citizen

A French citizen writes in a Rufisque newspaper to another citizen, his political adversary: "My uncle volunteered for the '70–'71 war. He served in the army of General Faidherbe, whom he had known as

Senegal's governor-general. He was wounded at Bapaume and evacuated to Senegal, where he died of bronchitis contracted on this European battlefield. Thus, my family is honorably and officially known. It has its place in the history of French colonization. Do remember it and ponder the old Wolof saying: 'Eggs don't fight stones.' "

This short document dates from 1931 and contains, in my view, these Senegalese traits: pride in being French and, at the same time, by old blood and a love for local arguments, pride in being Senegalese.

Dressed in their large national tunics or in well-fitted European suits; wearing shining patent leather shoes, the colonial helmet, dark glasses; a pencil behind the ear and a stick in hand; acting as if they were big bosses in front of Europeans, young Senegalese from the four communes offer easy targets for caricature. Mr. Blaise Diagne, black deputy [in the French National Assembly], now undersecretary to the colonies, does not hesitate to tell them that they have duties as well as rights and that they must work to deserve the honor of being citizens.

But it would be equally unjust not to notice what make them our equals. They share with us a desire for culture and learning, a devotion to their mother country, and the feeling of creating a larger France in Africa. However remarkable M. Diagne's case may be, it is not exceptional. It is stirring, but we also take it for granted.* Here is a Senegalese who became minister thanks to his intelligence and his will but also thanks to our institutions. He offers the best proof that France did not belie its principles, that it was right to adopt them. Diagne's success shows that a France encompassing several continents is not an empty promise.

The faults of the policy of assimilation can be mocked and denounced. It certainly makes the running of bureaucracy more difficult in that it is less authoritarian. Equally certain, however, is that when it succeeds it incomparably enhances the colony.

The still most solid element in AOF are the citizens of old Senegal. They are about 50,000, citizens in the four communes of Dakar, Saint-Louis, Gorée, and Rufisque, and are scattered in the ports or in the other colonies, where they are clerks, civil servants, or artisans. They represent about one-thirtieth of Senegal's population, one three-hundreths of the AOF population. But such figures do not have much meaning. Missions should not be judged according to the number of their catechumens nor should the strength of the French spirit in AOF be measured according to the number of Senegalese citizens. That this spirit becomes one with the republican mystique is a fact. The old cities, especially Saint-Louis and Gorée, still have among their inhabitants

*Blaise Diagne was the first black deputy from Senegal. He served in the French National Assembly from 1914 to his death in 1934. French liberals often pointed to him as an example of color blindness in French institutions (ed.).

ebony-faced republicans of long-standing for whom the Republic, the Revolution of '48, and Schoelcher* are not merely French symbols but, even more significant, Senegalese symbols as well.

Africans see for themselves that some Africans belong to France politically. They may think: why not us? It is very fortunate that they think in those terms. But aristocrats cry out. I realize that a policy of supremacy possesses a certain beauty. But the most noble aristocracies degenerate quickly if they do not have deep roots in the soil itself.

Today, we have too much faith in the good of economic success, material progress in the rational exploitation of the colonies. Of all the colonial empires of the past, I see only Rome and Portugal as having left their marks. What made Rome a great colonial power was its ability to give to the colonized populations the *jus latinum*. What made the Portuguese empire great was the practice of cross-breeding. In AOF, in Senegal, we are witnessing an intellectual cross-breeding, a *jus africanus*, an idea which has taken root and is stronger than many realize.

*Victor Schoelcher was an active abolitionist who in 1848, as undersecretary of naval affairs, signed the decree abolishing slavery in all French colonies. He subsequently became the symbol to black people of the humanitarian and idealist strain in the French empire. In addition to abolishing slavery, the Second Republic, established by the revolution of 1848, also extended to the Senegalese French citizenship (ed.).

Sources

1. *Petite histoire des colonies françaises* (Paris: Presses universitaires de France, 1944), pp. 5–7.

2. *Afrique occidentale française*, pp. 4–5, 150–51.

3. Louis Faivre [pseud.], "Aux temps des français," *Journal de débats*, July 26, 1931.

4. "Du dispensaire au grenier," *Temps*, January 15, 1932.

5. "La politique de Marius Moutet au ministère des colonies," *Actes du colloque Léon Blum, chef de gouvernement, 1936–1937* (Paris: Presses de la fondation nationale des sciences politiques, 1967), pp. 391–94.

6. "Les colonies dans la troisième république en 1939," *Vie intellectuelle* 13 (July 1945): 71–73, 79.

7. *Soudan-Paris-Bourgogne*, pp. 9–10.

8. "Equipe eurafricaine: Place pour l'allemagne?" *Esprit* 7 (November 1, 1938): 219, 225–27.

9. "Deutsche Mittelafrika?" *L'Europe nouvelle* (January 1, 1938): 16.

10. "Le bourgeois français au XIXe siècle et les colonies noires," *Afrique française* 45 (May 1935): 281–82.

11. "En AOF— Rapports et voeux," *Afrique française* 44 (October 1934): 585.

12. "Action colonisatrice et paysannat indigène," *Afrique française* 45 (1935): 529.

13. *Soudan-Paris-Bourgogne*, pp. 117, 121, 123–24, 126–29.

14. "L'esprit africain," *Afrique française* 63 (June 1933): 336.

15. *Afrique occidentale française*, pp. 24–25, 102.

16. *Toum*, pp. 134–37, 150–51.

17. "Connaissance des mentalités indigènes en AOF," *Congrès international et intercolonial de la société indigène, 5–10 Octobre 1931* (Paris, 1931), vol. 1: 553–56, 561–62, 566.

18. "La politique et l'administration indigènes en AOF," *Afrique française* 41 (January 1933): 9–11.

19. "En Afrique occidentale française—un homme nouveau: le chef indigène," *Temps*, June 4, 1931.

20. "Les Chefs noirs," *Temps*, September 10, 1931.

21. *Afrique occidentale française*, pp. 154–55.

22. "Le Dahomey à travers ses journaux," *Afrique française* 45 (April 1935): 233–35.

23. "Le Théatre de Gorée et la culture Franco-Africaine," *Afrique française* 47 (October 1937): 471–72.

24. *Afrique occidentale française*, pp. 159–60.

4   Colonial Reforms

After the Second World War France, like other European powers, increasingly found its power overseas curtailed and, in the face of growing nationalism, granted a series of reforms. A show of generosity, it was hoped, would more firmly link the overseas territories to the mother country. The French Union, made up of a federation of regions presumably equal in legal and political power, was proclaimed, but in fact the control from Paris never relaxed. The overseas territories constantly demanded increasing autonomy, and this insistence finally led to independence in 1960. While at times the demand for autonomy in Black Africa was heated and expressed itself in massive protest movements—and sometimes in violent uprisings such as that in Madagascar in 1947 and in the Cameroons in 1955—essentially the achievement of independence occurred in a gradual manner, especially when compared to the long and fierce colonial wars of Indochina and Algeria. This chapter is devoted to Delavignette's writings on the evolution of the overseas territories (particularly Black Africa) from the end of World War II to final independence in 1960.

Once France was liberated from German rule, Frenchmen began to think about drawing up a constitution for a new Republic, to be known as the Fourth Republic (to succeed the unhappy Third Republic, which had collapsed in 1940 as a result of German aggression). Writing in the autumn of 1945, Delavignette attempted to prescribe what the constitution of the Fourth Republic should include on the overseas territories. He noted the failures of the Third Republic in the colonial field and the need to grant equal legal and political rights to the overseas peoples, to integrate them politically into a French Union while still respecting their personalities and helping them evolve according to their own desires (1).

In this article and a number of others published in 1945 Delavignette attempted to show the extent to which Frenchmen in France had to cease thinking of the overseas people as mere dependents; the colonies were no longer possessions but rather extensions of France. Only if Frenchmen truly believed that the overseas people were their fellow citizens could a union based on harmony be established. Otherwise nationalism would triumph and the Union would dissolve (2, 3). Symbolizing the hoped-for symbiosis between the two cultures was Delavignette's dedication of the third essay to his friend, the Senegalese writer and poet Léopold Sédar Senghor, who in turn had earlier that year dedicated to Delavignette one of his writings.*

In 1951, speaking as the Lugard lecturer at the International African Institute in London, Delavignette attempted to compare the policies of his country with those of Britain. While Britain was leading its colonial people to freedom by an eventual grant of political independence, France, Delavignette asserted, was accomplishing the same feat by increasingly integrating the colonial peoples into the French political system (4). The speech was unusually optimistic in its assessment of the French Union, but nevertheless it did recognize that Africans increasingly would be deciding their own fate.

A few years after Delavignette's Lugard lecture, the African territories did increase their autonomous powers, and then in 1960—independence. A year later Delavignette wrote a quick survey of the evolution of the territories from 1946 to 1960. Prepared for a textbook published by the Alliance française, an educational institution promoting the teaching of French throughout the world, this description leaves out the shadows in the story of French decolonization and emphasizes France's positive accomplishments (5).

In 1960, writing for a more sophisticated audience, the Swiss *Revue économique et sociale*, Delavignette put the French experience of decolonization into the global perspective of the general loss of European empires (6). And writing retrospectively on the French experience in Africa in *L'Afrique noire française et son destin*, Delavignette considered how decolonization had become inevitable as a result of the failure in the interwar years to grant necessary reforms; those that had come subsequent to World War II were "too little and too late" (7). Looking at intellectual trends, he recognized that the empire had been held together by the haughty self-assurance of the nineteenth century; when that was undermined by self-doubt and cultural relativism, it was nearly inevitable that the empire would dissolve. The discovery of the

*"Vues sur l'Afrique noire, ou assimiler, non être assimilés," in *La Communauté impériale française* (Paris, 1945).

plurality of civilizations had sounded the death knell of empire (8).

As director of political affairs at the Ministry of Overseas France in the early years of the Fourth Republic, and in his writings, Delavignette was mainly concerned with the general outline of overseas reforms. But at a more practical level, he was instrumental in seeing these reforms implemented; from 1946 to 1947 he served as high commissioner of the Cameroons (that was the title of a governor in a mandate territory). In its attempt to extend French laws overseas and give the inhabitants of these areas some of the rights of the citizens of France proper, the Fourth Republic extended the rights to unionize and the protection of labor laws. To implement these reforms Delavignette as high commissioner formed a labor inspectorate (9). To help in the economic development of the Cameroons he also established vocational schools. The decree establishing one of them is reproduced here (10). But that was a very modest contribution; for the territory to be developed, a massive plan had to be implemented. Using the anniversary of August 27, 1940, the date on which the Cameroons declared for Free France, Delavignette announced ambitious economic plans, seeing in the prosperity of the Cameroons territorial liberation (11).

In speeches to the Representative Assembly in 1946 Delavignette extolled the generosity of the Fourth Republic, pointing out the political benefits given to the people of the Cameroons and the promise of economic development. With veiled references he tried to alert the European community in the Cameroons, pointing out that the era had changed, that it was necessary to adjust to the new world and to accept equality with those who formerly had been subjects (12, 13). Nearly thirty years later, writing in his memoirs, Delavignette recorded the nature of settler resistance and the manner in which he had forced the settlers to accept racial equality (14).

In his memoirs he also reveals the difficulty of his mission in the Cameroons and shows the extent to which his policies were shaped by the need to preserve the French mandate in an area considered difficult to control. Although he had announced to the Assembly the generosity of French political reforms, in his memoirs thirty years later Delavignette reveals the extent to which he was wracked by doubts about the wisdom of these reforms and recognized that they doomed his own power and role. Delavignette, who in the 1930s had asked for these reforms, had continued to urge France to implement them after World War II. The memoirs also show, ironically, a certain nostalgia for the authoritarianism which had belonged to the pre–World War II governors. It is a measure of his honesty and artistic ability that a generation later he was able to reproduce these fleeting thoughts (15).

1   The French Union
and the Constitution

"French Union" is a term coined by M. Giacobbi, Minister of the Colonies, during his governmental speech of March 25, 1945. This term designates the joining of the mother country and the overseas territories in a common political life.

Let us examine the situation as it was in 1939 and as it remained, mostly unchanged, at the beginning of 1945. We have to confront this situation if we want to give the French Union a constitution.

The overseas territories consist of different populations with varying political representation. In Algeria, which is under the control of the Ministry of the Interior, French citizens are represented on the same basis as those from France, whereas Tunisia and Morocco, which are supervised by the Foreign Office, have no representation of either French settlers or of natives.

Let us examine the territories which depend on the Ministry of the Colonies.

Nonfederated Colonies with Representation in Parliament

	Inhabitants	Representatives	Senators
Martinique and Guadeloupe	501,000	4	2
Guiana	32,000	1	—
East Indian possessions	290,000	1	1
Réunion Island	328,000	2	1
	1,151,000	8	4

Federated Colonies with Representation in Parliament

Senegal (3 communes)*	1 representative
Cochinchina	1 representative

Senegal is part of the Federation of French West Africa, and Cochinchina of the Indochinese Union. Only French citizens can vote in these two territories, and the natives who are French citizens represent a fraction of the native population as a whole.

Colonies with No Representation in Parliament

These consist of all those colonies which have not yet been mentioned: Madagascar; French Equatorial Africa (Gabon, the Congo, Oubangui, Chad); French West Africa (those parts of Senegal which have no voting rights, Guinea, Ivory Coast, Dahomey, Mauritania, Sudan, Niger); Indochina (the section which cannot vote and which comprises most of Cochinchina, most of Tonkin, the protectorates of Cambodia, Laos,

*Goree and Dakar were merged into a single commune in 1929 (ed.).

Annam); Somaliland; New Caledonia; Pacific establishments; and Saint
Pierre and Miquelon.

In a word, almost 50 million inhabitants, whether they be French
citizens like our 15,000 settlers from New Caledonia or natives, have no
voting rights. And we should add that territories under mandate are not
represented either.

Can we now view the problem confronting us? Generally speaking,
we are confronted with three broad types of territories: colonies (some of
which are federated), protectorates, and mandates. Three different
ministries are involved: the Ministry of Foreign Affairs, the Ministry of
the Interior, and the Ministry of Colonies. We distinguish five groups:
voting citizens, nonvoting citizens, natives who are colonial subjects,
natives who are French "protected individuals" (in the protectorates),
and natives governed by the French (in territories under mandate).

Thus, except for the parliamentary representatives of the Algerian
settlers there are only ten deputies and four senators to represent the
West Indies, Réunion, Guiana, some communes of Senegal, and some
regions of Cochinchina.

The rest—and this means 60 million inhabitants! [sic]—live under a
regime which permits the concentration of executive and legislative
powers in one minister's hands.

Such a regime cannot endure. But we should now examine the
difficulties inherent in its transformation.

Millions of men who should enjoy this right have no representatives.
How can we make this happen? Some say all there is to do is simply to
apply to the overseas people the rules applied in the mother country. Did
not the Second Republic do just this in 1848, and did it not make the
colonies of the times into departments or administrative units like those
of France?

But, when we stop to think, we realize that significant differences exist
between the situation of the colonies in 1848 and that of the French Union
in 1945. Then, the problem was to include less than a million men into
French political life. Today, it is on another scale, for we are not dealing
with one million but several million men and women who have to be
brought into the political arena. We should also note, and this is much
more important, that numbers are not the only new element. We now are
dealing with diverse individuals and personal conditions which can no
longer be ignored. People enjoy Moslem status* in North Africa and
large sections of Black Africa; Annamite and Cambodian statuses in
Indochina; Hova status in Madagascar. And racial awareness is spread-

*The legal right of the natives to live under their own laws, such as local family
and property laws, was guaranteed by statute, and this constituted their
"status" (ed.).

ing among yellow as well as black peoples. Furthermore, political matters differ fundamentally in Asia, Africa, and Europe's France, and they present obstacles to the establishment of a representative system.

We should not deny the existence of these differences; we should study them. Instead of strangling them by imposing a false uniformity, we should carefully take into account the racial identities and the Asian, African, and Malagasy situations when looking for a system which will allow their representation in the French Union.

To acknowledge present difficulties is not to deny the feasibility of political representation. There are two types of difficulties: technical and political.

By technical difficulties, I mean those stemming from the fact that many populations do not read. For example, French West Africa has only about 500 schools, which are attended by 60,000 students, whereas the population at large is 15 million. Such a situation is the more serious if we realize that only seven young Africans want to become school-teachers this year. If our educational efforts fail, on what solid basis can we hope to establish political representation? Can we establish freedom without schools and schoolteachers? Let us not delve further into this painful matter, but let us keep in mind that it is present everywhere, in North Africa as well as in Black Africa and in Indochina. Action should be taken immediately. We are told about prestige. Let us begin by opening schools and encouraging youth to become dedicated teachers. Prestige cannot exist without education.

By political difficulties, I mean those due to the existence of the racial identities and personal conditions which I have mentioned. To illustrate this point, let us take an example from Africa. For a long time, to become a French citizen was the highest political goal of a black from West Africa. To vote and be a citizen like the Senegalese from the communes was the hope and ambition of men from Dahomey, Sudan, or the Ivory Coast. I am not certain that this is still the case today. People may still want to become citizens but not at the expense of their personal status, which is often Moslem, or at the expense of their awareness as Africans and as Blacks. French citizenship will not now be used to achieve imitation of the mother country but to assert black and African identity. I do not think that this is bad; on the contrary I approve of it. We should realize fully that the French Union will not be the extension of our domestic institutions and values overseas. It will be the locus where civilizations meet, and some of these civilizations will startle us by their originality and their vitality. It will not mean the expansion of our old Republic but the eruption of new nationalisms into our homes.

Some nationalist movements and some cultures will want to be represented in the French Union in order to have a forum in which to express their Asian or African raison d'être. If such a condition is met, they will then search for a raison d'être common to them and to us, in a French Union superior to them and to us and one which will, I hope, give birth to a new, organic entity.

But we should emphasize that, if such a union is to be achieved, we must not take the easiest road and mistake uniformity for unity. It would not be too difficult, under the pretext of preserving Jacobin unity, to mold a uniform Republic in all five regions of the world where France is present. We could also easily give seats in the Paris parliament to more "colonial" representatives than in the past. But such an action would quickly prove ineffective.

In fact, Moslems from North Africa, blacks from Africa and Malagasy, Annamites and people from the Far East are infinitely more varied than were Frenchmen from the different provinces prior to 1789. These men, and I cannot stress it too strongly, do have their own civilizations, their Asian or African personal awareness (and such an awareness is often a religious one), the feeling of being black or yellow. They do not want to relinquish any part of their personalities in order to blend into a falsely uniform system which would be no more than a caricature of the democratic Republic. Industrialization in their countries and the increase of material and cultural exchanges, however, may modify this spirit and push them faster toward us.

But we should go toward them and recognize them for what they are. Under these conditions we will build the French Union with them, and together we will give birth to an organically unified France throughout the world.

Is not the secret formula for human brotherhood a synthesis of African, Asian, American, Oceanic, and European elements? France has all these elements in her hands.

Instead of trying to give prominence, more or less unconsciously, to the European element above the others, let us blend them all in this French Union which will be the melting pot for our new unity. All countries, not only the mother country, will be penetrated by the new spirit. We cannot yet imagine what this new French unity will be, a unity which will resound with all the songs from different parts of the world in fullest realization of our humanity.

2   French Colonization on Trial

I am aware that in North Africa, Black Africa, Madagascar, and Indochina our colonization is subject to grave criticism. But what is questioned? Is it the ideal of human perfectibility and unity, or our incapacity to materialize economic and political structural reforms? I know that we are blamed for proclaiming this ideal but not acting on it. Finally, I understand that we are being accused of no longer believing in what we advocate.

This situation creates an advantage for the African and Asian nationalists. They point to the discrepancy between our ideals and our ability to act, our mystique and our policy. But if we practice with confidence a real policy of human unity, based on representation and exchanges between all the different parts of the French world, we will be able to gather in the same community groups which will keep their own characteristics and which will, according to Paul Valéry,* enrich one another, thanks to these mutual differences. This is the meaning of our colonization.

There will be no more colonies in the old sense of territories dependent on the mother country; there will be a French union of countries which will encourage human unity through cultural interchange that comes from cross-colonization. To colonize is to cultivate man.

But all nationalists—whether white, yellow, or black—will ask, why a union? Can we not ensure intellectual and material exchanges by means other than working within a community? The answer is no. To produce in great quantities, to equip a laboratory, to electrify primitive rural areas in French Africa and backward ones in European France, we have to live and work together.

When, through war, we have experienced the death of the old world and witnessed the fragility of the human condition, we can reaffirm life and the basic unity of men by joining varied peoples with one another in the building of a new world. The different provinces of France are everywhere in the world, under the name of mother country, colonies, protectorates, and mandated territories. They offer a complete collection of the human species. Are we going to miss this opportunity to create a synthesis?

We in European France will have to become workers who associate, physically and intellectually, with black and yellow comrades within the French Union. Maybe we will have to be paid the same wages in order to build the city whose judicial form is still unknown but whose purpose will not be to serve a few privileged men. For the heart of the matter is to work together, knowing for whom we work. For investment companies? Or for a France composed of workers who symbolize human dignity?

Those who do not believe in a program of social work with black and yellow people, who do not believe that it is possible to renew the concept of humanism through *communion* with them—are they skeptical about human perfectibility and unity? Then they should prepare themselves for

*A twentieth-century French writer whose universal humanism inspired Delavignette (ed.).

a harsher poverty and a stronger feeling of isolation than they experienced during the Nazi occupation. But the world will be rebuilt nevertheless, without them.

Popular opinion that identifies overseas France as only an offshoot of France itself causes a separation between ourselves and African or Asian France and a blow to our ideal of unity. We do not protest, then, as landowners threatened by expropriation or merchants faced by bankruptcy; we protest because something much more important than a business or an estate may be taken away from us. Those who do not share our faith are trying to destroy our confidence that we can strengthen our unity by enriching it through exchanges with Asia and Africa. They want to deprive us not only of a patrimony but also of the task that requires us to unite with other races and to renew ourselves.

I believe that this renewal consists not in denying humanism but in rediscovering it for our world of machines and masses. To lose faith in our perfectibility and in our unity would be to commit suicide.

3   The French Union
To Léopold Sédar Senghor

When the colonies were made by and for the mother country, the latter enjoyed the life-style of an owner vis-à-vis the colonies. The landowner could be good or bad but was above all the owner. France could use and even abuse the colonies. She forced them to trade solely with her, to give their raw materials to her only, and to become a market for French products in preference to those of other nations. She could forbid the colonies to create local industries, to transform and exploit their raw materials in their own countries. And the mother country could sell her colonies. She behaved overseas like a European landowner in a foreign land.

When the colonies reached a certain development and when, by expressing their desire to join France and even to become an integral part of France, they colored the union with an Asian or African imprint, the mother country's right as owner became less important and less European. The life-style enjoyed by the mother country was very different from that of the colonies and had to change. An idea which is spreading is that the mother country and her colonies should organize in order to live *together*, to erect a community where very different peoples will be able to serve *together* common moral and material interests, working *together* to make a better future. The landowner and his property exist no more; they have been replaced by the former owner and his former sharecroppers, all of whom are searching for a new life-style that will allow them to develop what was the property of one, a property

that has now become common to all and superior to all. This property
now owned in common encompasses not only the colonies but also the
mother country.

Such a union is the opposite of domination. It will force the mother
country to modify not only her life-style but also her way of thinking.
We can no longer think of the ancient Roman Empire; it is not now a
question of exercising force over men. To implant in the concept of the
French Union any thought of dominating our overseas populations, of
dominating men called natives in order to distinguish them from the
colonial settlers and officials, would be false and pernicious. *Tomorrow,
we all will be the natives of the same French Union.*

In everyday life, we will be in contact with Moslems, Buddhists,
animists. This is already the case but we are not aware of it. The Union
will make us realize the existence of new social links, of a new and total
human solidarity. To say that these Moslems, Buddhists, animists are
our brothers will not be enough; we will have to accept the fact that more
and more they will be able to participate politically in running the
community they form with us.

According to Léopold Sédar Senghor, in *La Communauté impériale
française*, Africans want "to assimilate, not to be assimilated"; they want
to assimilate themselves. Together we shall seek common motives for
living with one another. They invite us to participate in a task and fulfill
an ideal which we will find true to our traditions.

If we give up the concept of the French Union, if we let the colonies live
by means of expedients, and go on talking of colonies and thinking in
colonial terms rather than in terms of union, then we will betray it, we
will be turning our backs to the future and to new ways of life.

4   The British and French Ways
in Africa

Great Britain and France have been working for about a century in Black
Africa, exploring and developing the southern and central portions of
this enormous continent. Where do they stand in relationship to one
another and to Africa itself? What have they each achieved through their
long efforts? After a colonial period during which the two European
nations at times clashed on African roads as bitter rivals and at other
times emulated one another and generously cooperated, what is their
African future? These are very important questions.

British policy has just been strongly asserted in the Gold Coast.* It
evolves in the same fashion in Nigeria, Sierra-Leone, and Gambia. I do

*In 1950 the British allowed the devolution of executive powers to Africans.
Kwame Nkrumah became prime minister in 1951 (ed.).

not have to describe it to you. You are familiar with it. This policy acknowledges that the Crown's former colonies are independent within the framework of the Commonwealth. Already in Accra African ministers assist an African prime minister, one of his country's nationalist leaders. The British governor's powers are being diminished. This in turn will modify the administrative structure of the civil service. I do not have to emphasize these formidable facts since you are well aware of them.

But allow me to present in greater detail the French policy in Western Africa, in Equatorial Africa since the 1946 Constitution, and in the territories under trusteeship, Togo and the Cameroons.

In order to understand this policy, we have to understand the goals which define it and the means which characterize it.

The goals are stated in the constitution of the Fourth Republic approved by the 1946 referendum. AOF and AEF are integral parts of the French Republic, which encompasses the departments of the mother country and the overseas territories. The means are those prescribed by our internal laws. They consist of two essentially representative systems: one in Paris on the national level and the other in Africa on the regional level.

The African territories that are part of the French Republic are represented in our national political institutions. Twenty-seven representatives from Black Africa, of whom twenty-three are natives, have seats in the National Assembly. According to French law, they not only represent the African district that elected them but also France as a whole. Thus a black deputy can influence through his vote pieces of legislation which in fact concern the mother country more than Africa, or do not apply to himself at all. Insofar as laws change mores, our black representatives, through their legislative powers deeply affect our lives.

We find African representatives in other bodies in Paris as well: the Council of the Republic has thirty-three African senators, of whom nineteen are natives; the Assembly of the French Union has forty African members, of whom twenty-nine are natives. There is also in Africa a type of regional representation that takes place at the territorial and municipal levels.

To complete the picture, we should note two essential facts. The first one is that penal justice is the same throughout the union; it is no longer dealt to Africans through special courts different from those reserved for Europeans. The second fact is that all Africans are French citizens. Here I ask your close attention, for I want to put to rest a frequent misunderstanding.

We are told that by bestowing citizenship on Africans we assimilate them. I deny this, since they can, if they wish, retain their private civil statuses. Assimilation does not take place now as it did under the former

French policy of 1848, which was exercised in the West Indies, in
Réunion, and in Guiana. We witness the integration of a community of
persons who enjoy different civil statuses. A Moslem and a fetichist have
the same civil liberties and the same political rights as a Frenchman from
the mother country whose status is determined by the civil code.

Great Britain and France have each operated in Africa according to an
internal logic or, if you prefer, to an internal lack of logic. These two
nations, who hold in common the democratic ideal but who understand
democracy in their own ways, have been directly or indirectly teachers of
freedom.

Great Britain democratizes Africa by giving it the means to construct
new nations that will have their places in the Commonwealth. France
grants the African citizenship within the Republic, within the national
community which in turn is modified by the African who brings with
him his personal status.

Great Britain enlarges her community of nations in order to take
Africa into the fold. France alters the very essence of her national
structure in order to grant citizenship to her former African subjects and
to integrate African regionalism into the Republic.

These two policies are very different but they share a common and
deep concern for African identity. Both contribute to the making of a
new Africa, which through a commonwealth in the British fashion or
citizenship in the French manner, will play its role in the world of
tomorrow.

How will this new Africa act? I am no fortune-teller so I can only
prophesy by relying on the past.

In the colonial past of Africa, Europeans of the stature of Lord Lugard
could exercise a great influence. Such a man could bring about profound
change by virtue of his strong personality and his capacity for hard
work. Slavery could be abolished on the African continent by a powerful
European governor. Lord Lugard proved it was possible.

Perhaps in the Africa of tomorrow conditions will no longer allow
English or French men to effect social change. This is not only because
African peoples will be led more and more by Africans but because the
time when great personalities left their mark has probably ended and will
be replaced by a period where masses will have more importance than
individuals, in Africa as everywhere else in the world.

Nevertheless the spirit which was Lord Lugard's will not disappear. I
hope it will inspire the makers of the emerging African society.

5 Twelve Years of Reforms

As early as 1946, just after the German occupation, France, free again, implemented a policy whose originality can clearly be seen in Black Africa and in Madagascar.

It has been said that the aim of the policy was assimilation and that it thus followed the rational French spirit, which ignored African and Malagasy characteristics in order to blend everything in a universality which it called civilization.

Historical truth is a good deal more subtle. Yes, in 1946 France gave to all her nationals from Black Africa and Madagascar French citizenship and the related civil rights which only her old colonies from the West Indies, Guiana, and Réunion, and the four Senegalese communes, had been enjoying since the 1848 revolution. Indeed we could call this policy assimilation. But—and this can never be overemphasized—France did not make the adoption of her code a prerequisite for citizenship. African and Malagasy people were naturalized within their own civil statutes. The fact that they became citizens did not force them to relinquish their customary institutions regarding persons and property. This was not assimilation; quite the contrary.

We then witnessed in Black Africa and in Madagascar a political phenomenon whose originality and force were often not reported by confounded observers. Hundreds of thousands of new citizens rushed into French political life and modified the composition of the electorate, the parliament, and the French government. A few figures will demonstrate clearly. Before 1946, in French West Africa, only four Senegalese communes voted, and they elected a representative who, in 1913,* would be a black from Dakar. In 1946, there were 500,000 voters in AOF; by the 1958 referendum there were 10,200,000. Between 1946 and 1958, Black Africa and Madagascar added about 15 million voters—male and female—to the mother country's 27 million. During these twelve years, the sixty-three overseas representatives in the National Assembly (without mentioning the senators) played a role in shaping the future of France. It became customary to include African ministers who sometimes were Muslims. What figures cannot express is the great human quality which accompanied the African and Malagasy rising on the French political scene—Mauritanian camel herders, Fulani cattle rangers, black peasants from the Sudanese Savannah, and plantation owners from the west coast of Africa. Malagasy rice growers became accustomed to voting. Since most of them were illiterate, a symbol was used to represent their candidates. We should not smile: they thus entered a network of human relationships that allowed them to communicate with European Frenchmen.

As important to the community's direction was the April 30, 1946, law which created the fund for overseas economic and social development. It

*He means 1914 (ed.).

introduced in legislation and in public opinion a new concept of financial and technical assistance to these underdeveloped countries which, prior to 1946, had no one to rely on except themselves. From 1946 to 1958, their equipment was financed through loans without security, which were in fact gifts and which came from the partial redistribution of the GNP of the mother country. Although impoverished by occupation, France spent in 1946 for her former colonies a sum which in proportion to national income was larger than that given by any other nation to underdeveloped countries in 1958. The principle of solidarity was applied even before the community came into being. The French mother country knows that colonies no longer exist and that, beneath the old names, poor countries continue in existence which do not constitute a treasure to be taken or an estate to be exploited but a burden to be equitably shared in an atmosphere of solidarity.

An essential fact to note is that each French territory, from 1946 to 1958, was granted its own representative assembly. In 1957 these assemblies were elected through universal suffrage, and they controlled the autonomous government which was established for each territory. Thus, two strong pillars of democracy—the legislative and the executive branches—were installed in Black Africa and in Madagascar at the territorial level. Some people rightly said that in Black Africa, if not in Madagascar, each territory had been arbitrarily cut out during the colonial period. Today, however, we notice that independent, modern Africa uses the colonial configuration spontaneously for its young republics and that the *colonial territory*, far from being an administrative entity imposed from the outside, has in fact become an African reality.

In short, from 1946 to 1958, twelve years of reforms transformed French Black Africa and Madagascar more deeply than fifty years of colonization and centuries of precolonial life. This important task was silently being carried out while the wars in Indochina (1945–54) and Algeria (as of 1954) were making headlines.

The community was founded in 1958. Its vital principle was the equality and solidarity of the nations that joined voluntarily. Which nations were they? Eleven territories from Black Africa and Madagascar, through the 1958 September referendum, expressed their desire to form with the French Republic, their former mother country, a community. This was an *open* community, each state being free to leave when it so desired. In 1960, Sudan, after trying unsuccessfully to form a federation with Senegal, left the community and became the Mali Republic.

During that same year, the legal structure upon which the community was built underwent important modifications. The 1958 community was characterized by a sharing of powers dealing with military defense, diplomacy, currency, and economic development. These powers were transferred, in 1960, [to insure independence] to each African state and to the Malagasy state, with all of which the French Republic signed agreements to cooperate. What these accords shared is the fact that the African and Malagasy republics have been recognized as sovereign states which deal and cooperate with France on an equal footing.

The French Community established in 1958* can, in certain respects, be viewed as a transitory compromise between the responsibilities that France wanted to assume towards overseas states and the aspirations of nations which want France's help without too much interference in their affairs. We realize, of course, that this compromise is denounced by those who advocate an immediate and complete independence, as well as by those who, nostalgically, remember the days when imperial sovereignty spread from Algiers to Dakar, from Brazzaville to Saigon and Tananarive and included the Tunisian and Moroccan protectorates.

But the spirit of cooperation which will inspire the community operates on a world scale and is oriented toward the future. Throughout the world, in all countries, two tendencies clash: one pushing for a planetary unification achieved by the union of man and technology, the other driving each country toward an independence which strengthens national characteristics. May the community harmonize these two tendencies by giving its people hope for a great common future. It is not at all a matter of amiably settling a colonial past. More is involved than merely giving technical and financial assistance and then working for a higher standard of living. It involves the emergence of a new life-style, of a new art of living among diverse peoples who will, as Paul Valéry said, share a desire to enrich themselves through their differences.

6 The Colonial Policies of
European Powers since 1945

In order to understand fully the colonial policies of the European states since 1945, the international context in which they operated should be examined. There were only five colonial powers: Belgium, France, Great Britain, the Netherlands, and Portugal. All but Portugal had suffered from the Second World War. None of them, not even Portugal, could ignore the international situation. The importance of the international context for colonial policy was a fundamental, new concept which emerged during the two world wars and was clearly visible in 1945. All colonial powers, except Portugal, adhered to the charter of the United

*As of 1961, when this essay was published, it was not fully realized that the community established in 1958 had not only been transformed by the full achievement of independence by the African territories but in fact had been destroyed (ed.).

Nations which was signed in San Francisco on June 26, 1945. The eleventh article of the charter declared that the signatories would develop the capacity of the colonized people for self-government, and the twelfth article provided for an international system of trust territories. The African countries under mandate were as early as 1946 placed under the system of trusteeship, which opened the road to independence. And all the colonies or protectorates could refer to the San Francisco Charter as giving them the right to develop their own political aspirations. We realize that this marks the end of colonial empires as built or perfected by nineteenth-century Europe. It indicates also the end of the colonial era, when problems stemming from colonization were internal ones that each mother country could solve according to its own spirit, either through sovereign power or through confrontation or dialogue with its territories.

After World War II three world powers emerged on the international scene. They pooled their efforts in order to speed up the liquidation begun by the San Francisco Charter.

In the name of "universal democracy" the United States challenged the colonial edifices as if they were decrepit houses not fit for living in which should be demolished in order to make way for avenues of progress. Did the Americans think of their own independence and identify with the colonial struggle for emancipation? Or is it that they believed that what was good for them was good for all? They would not have understood if we had objected that civilizations had developed and could reappear in Asia and in Africa on principles which differed greatly from those they advocated.

In the name of "Marxist-Leninist socialism," the Soviet Union attacked European colonization as "tainted by capitalism." The roads to Paris and Western Europe passed through Peking and Asia; they soon would pass through Africa too. The multinational USSR used Asian and African nationalisms to undermine colonial empires.

Thus the U.S. and the Soviet Union were two giants competing as advocates of decolonization.

Last, in the name of Christianity, the Catholic and Protestant churches proclaimed that the yearnings for independence expressed by colonized nations were legitimate. Christianity did not want to appear bound to colonialism. Nationalism appeared in Asia and also in Africa well before 1945, acquiring strength at the time of the Second World War; it was also a very important element of the international context in which colonialism struggled. Asia and Africa were no longer stagnant; their masses were on the move, appearing on the world stage which Europe no longer monopolized. Asia and Africa are poor. But this poverty constituted in their eyes an argument in favor of independence. In what way? First of all, let us note that none of the European colonies in Asia and Africa were rich in comparison with their respective mother countries (as Latin American territories are, compared to Spain and Portugal). But Asia and Africa claim to have been exploited by colonialism, and they doubt its ability to better their economies through planning. Planning indeed implies to the African an undisputed political authority which the African feels cannot come from the outside. Only Asian or African nationals will be allowed to exercise such a power.

We must emphasize the fact that colonies were no longer isolated and that what affected one, no matter where it was located in the world, had an effect on the others.

Setting aside for now the cases of Belgium and Portugal, let us examine the two great colonial powers of the nineteenth century: Great Britain and France.

In 1945, the Labor government declared that the goal of British policy was "to guide colonial territories toward self-government within the Commonwealth, in such a way that a high standard of living as well as assurances against any type of oppression can be provided."

These ideas were already present in British thinking before 1945 in the person of Lord Lugard. He viewed colonization as a double mandate: to spread British dominion and to lead natives toward self-government, which meant in fact to turn the empire into a commonwealth in which the members would be internally autonomous. This double concept of commonwealth and self-government characterized British policy and gathered momentum after 1945.

What does this term "Commonwealth" represent? It is difficult to define in terms of constitutional law. The term does not refer to a constitution but to an institution which has its roots in imperial and colonial traditions but is not an empire any longer. The Commonwealth can be said to be typically British because of the well-measured mixture of practicality and idealism. It is open to an infinite variety of peoples and civilizations, encompassing 650 million men all over the world. It works, it has been said, on the principle of the Round Table around which King Arthur's descendants sit on an equal footing with the various representatives from more or less democratic regimes. Is it bound to the sterling pound? No, Canada belongs to the dollar zone. Is it predominantly white and European? No, two of its population masses—India and Pakistan—are Asian. In short, if it is difficult to say what the Commonwealth is, it is easy to say what it is not. It is not a federation and has no federal institutions. It comprises states which are federated without being a federation.

What do the British mean by self-government? It is here perhaps that we find the greatest innovation of British colonial policy; it is no longer restricted to internal autonomy. Rather, full independence occurred, beginning in 1947 in Asia and in 1957 in Africa when dominion status was granted. It had first been proposed for Canada in 1839, and then carried out in 1867; instituted for Australia in 1900, for New Zealand in 1907, and South Africa in 1910. It seemed to be an act of emancipation of European communities found to have reached maturity and whose common bond was their allegiance to the Crown of England. Then, beginning in Asia in 1947 and in Africa in 1957, dominions of color received full equality with the white dominions and the insistence on allegiance to the Crown was accommodated: the republic of India was freed from allegiance to the British monarchy and recognized Her Britannic Majesty only as head of the Commonwealth.

We could say that the Commonwealth is a circle of free nations which bring into the Commonwealth the ideal of cooperation; this cooperation helps produce social progress that would be unattainable if the nations were alone. Although they do not interfere with one another's cultures, they undoubtedly are bound by a de facto interdependence which allows India, for example, to influence Great Britain and vice versa.

How shall we characterize French policy? Taking into account the fact that such divisions are inherently arbitrary, we can divide French policy into three periods.

The first period, from the Brazzaville Conference in January–February of 1944 to the establishment of the constitution of the Fourth Republic in October 1946, saw a compromise between the old colonial system and attempts at reforms, some of which sprang from a spirit of federalism and others from a centralist attitude.

In the mother country, then occupied by German invaders, the overseas empire never shone more brilliantly. As the seat of the Free French government in 1942, it represented free French land. It became an asset of the greatest importance for the hero of Free France, General de Gaulle. Lack of knowledge about the colonies helped build the imperial myth. France, freed in 1944–45 in part as a result of the help of the empire, could not believe that this very imperial effort would lead to the dissolution of the empire. Frenchmen favored reforms but they did not think there would be an abandonment of the colonies. Reforms had been advocated during the Brazzaville Conference. Far from foreseeing the colonies evolving toward self-government, the conference excluded this development even as a long-term goal; it denounced self-government as being opposed to the civilizing goals set by France for the overseas territories.

In the autumn of 1946, the constitution of the Fourth Republic marked the beginning of the second period, which lasted until 1957. This period is characterized by the establishment of a united French Republic that incorporated the populations of its former African and Malagasy empire while also granting associated status to the Indochinese states. These states and the French Republic constituted the French Union. But—and this is a vital new element—the French Republic was no longer what it was before 1939. It now consisted of France and her overseas departments: West Indies, Réunion Island and Guiana; to this we should add the immense colonies from Africa and Madagascar as well as establishments in India and in the South Sea Islands and New Caledonia. To add further complexity to this makeup, we should note the trustee territories, Togo and the Cameroons, which were considered associated territories.

Let us examine this state of integration which we cannot name but which indeed existed, de facto as well as de jure, for twelve years, from 1946 to the basic law of 1956 and to the birth of the Fifth Republic in 1958.

From 1946 on, all nationals from overseas countries other than Indochina were French citizens. The May 7, 1946, law, which was confirmed by the October 1946 constitution, granted these nationals French citizenship without in any way depriving them of their personal civil statute.

Never before, and I should stress this fact, had the French Republic extended itself so extensively overseas, especially in Africa. What guided the makers of the 1946 constitution? What principles supported such attempts at universality? How could they break away from the long-standing doctrine of the civil code, which required for naturalization the acceptance of the civil code? How could they declare that peoples whose civilizations and structures were so heterogeneous could group together under the same political sovereignty? Did they wish to reenact in the twentieth century the Caracalla edict?* Did they fear that the Brazzaville Conference would lead to self-government and prefer to make French citizens out of overseas nationals instead of granting autonomy to the various territories?

In the French national assembly and in the other political bodies, the elected African representatives did experience a form of self-government. The Fourth Republic set up in each territory a local assembly, the functions of which increased rapidly and for which independence eventually would become a goal.

Before proceeding, let us underline the importance of the April 30, 1946, law which asked the taxpayer of the mother country to finance the social and economic infrastructure in the overseas regions of the French Republic. For 12 years, the overseas territories received 2.5 percent of France's yearly national revenue. No country, to my knowledge, provided so large an amount of foreign aid.

*This edict, named after the third century A.D. Roman emperor, granted virtually all inhabitants of the Roman empire citizenship (ed.).

The third period started in 1956 with Gaston Defferre's basic law,*
which broke ground for the present community. The territorial assemblies were given more power. Their functions were essentially legislative.
They chose or elected African governments whose powers equalled those
of the French governor. Thus the two key elements of self-government,
the executive and the legislative branches, were now present. In October
1958 more of the overseas territories of the French Republic became
autonomous states, then African republics, and a Malagasy Republic was
formed on the basis of equality with the French Republic. Thus a new entity was created, the *Community*. On April 4, 1960, this new Community
changed drastically. The Malagasy Republic and the Federation of Mali,
which consisted of Senegal and Sudan, signed agreements with the
French Republic as sovereign states.

Here is my conclusion, which is only conjecture.
First, the decolonization which took place south of the Sahara seemed
to the former European powers as natural as colonization seemed in the
nineteenth century. This process was seen as tightly linked to the
ex-colonies' independence. Decolonization seemed to the Europeans to be
imperfect as long as independence was not complete. Second, the fact
that the ex-colonies are independent does not exempt the former mother
countries from helping these countries build their social and economic
infrastructures, according to agreements freely negotiated on the basis of
full equality between the former colonies and the mother country.
Finally, I want to note two unknowns. The first one is the Algerian
problem, which is outside my topic since it lies north of the Sahara. But
how can we not perceive that Algeria can no more be disconnected from
Africa than from France! The second one is the South African Union.
How can we fail to see in the Bantu question one of the keys to the future
of all Africa?

7   Lost Opportunities

From the Rhine River to the Congo via the Atlas Mountains, the Sahara
Desert, Senegal, and Niger, from temperate zones to tropical and
equatorial regions, France in conjunction with French Africa compares
geographically to the vast Russian and North American continents.
Could we not see there a Eurafrican block linked by the Mediterranean?

*The French Parliament, unwilling to take on the responsibility of lessening
French control overseas, promulgated a "basic law" which gave the minister of
Overseas France, Gaston Defferre, the authority to establish in the overseas
territories governments which would be responsible to the locally elected
territorial assemblies. These assemblies were now elected by universal rather
than by limited suffrage (ed.).

Pacified, the Sahara no longer divided Europe and Africa. Thus, did not everything converge to make French Africa, closely connected to France, the vital center for a great policy which would no longer be colonial in the old narrow meaning of the word? The answer to the rhetorical question, history tells us, is no.

Now that these dreams have, like illusions, vanished, we can understand better what missing elements prevented them from being realized. French Africa represented a bloc on paper only. In reality, this African unity was not without cracks. Making a French Eurafrica implied building foundations, and few men could, morally and technically, do this. Without copying England and its Commonwealth or the Soviet Union, France and Africa could have joined into a multinational union or a federal state.

The French and African peoples were separated less by distance than by living conditions and especially by a mutual ignorance of one another which kept them far apart. The French always felt they were superior to the Negro-African man. Fundamentally, the mother country looked at Africa with a prejudice which ignored all scientific research and stifled curiosity about Black Africa. These black people, were not they "overgrown children"?

Between 1919 and 1939, all the elements and opportunities to build a great French Eurafrican policy were present in both North Africa and Black Africa. But World War II was to break out on a France which had limited herself to mouthing idealistic imperial slogans while carrying out a very conservative policy in colonial matters.

8   The Death Knell of Colonialism

Our grandfathers did not doubt the legitimacy of civilizing African populations whom they thought barbaric; to them the Machine Hall Exposition of 1889 symbolized the virtue of a universal civilizing mission. Ironically, this very progress that colonization had introduced in Africa was ultimately to turn against Europe. Progress and colonization had allowed anthropologists to work safely with means that explorers did not possess; the results of their research renewed the concept of classical humanism. Mankind was characterized by a plurality of civilizations, among which none, in law as well as fact, could claim to be unique. Peoples that were thought to be backward—half-witted or retarded, the Belgians said—surprised us, when examined in a primitive, prelogical frame of reference, by their intricate and rich institutions which were finally unearthed and scraped from the realm of the exotic where they had been confined. The sciences of man disqualified the simplistic distinction between superior and inferior civilizations as well as the neat division of our planet into civilizing peoples and peoples to be civilized. "We now know that as civilizations we are mortal." These words by Paul Valéry also mean: we now know that as civilizations we are not one but many.

The self-assurance which had inspired European colonization and helped so many men in the bush disintegrated. The Japanese victory over Russia in 1905 rang a knell which very few of us heard. The numerous deaths that marked World War I were not seen in their relationship to Europe's colonial future at the time. The great shock which we did feel, however, came from the discovery of the plurality of civilizations.

9 High Commissioner of the Cameroons
Labor Inspectors

Article 1: Labor department inspectors in the Cameroons work within the general framework set up by the August 17, 1944, decree.

Article 2: Labor Department inspectors should visit all firms, companies, and farms set up in the Cameroons, whatever their nature and whoever the employer, public or private, secular or religious. The inspection covers all workers, whatever their legal status or sex.

Any person who gives his services for money, whatever his position and whatever the duration, is called a worker.

All trainees, whether they are paid or not, are also called workers.

Article 3: The labor department inspector's role is
a) to see that the laws governing working conditions and workers' protection are applied;
b) to carry out surveys and studies as planned by the laws.
c) to help develop, through their advice, lasting rapport between employers and employees and to maintain social harmony;
d) to keep the administration informed about the worker's condition;
e) to formulate advice and suggestions about measures which could better the worker's lot and to prepare the necessary documents for the carrying out of such suggestions; and
f) to study all questions pertaining to social matters which shall be submitted to them.

10 High Commissioner of the Cameroons
A Vocational School

The goal of the Douala vocational school is to train industrial technicians for various administrative departments and for private industry. The school depends on the education service for its direction, organization, and pedagogical control.

The school has four sections:

1. woodwork: joinery, cabinetmaking, carpentry, cartwrights;
2. metalwork: machine fitting, turning, boilermaking, ironworks, tool sharpening, auto mechanics;
3. public service section: roads and buildings;
4. electrical section.

The curriculum will last four years. The subjects to be taught, the schedules, the examinations, and the graduation procedure will be determined by a forthcoming regulation.

European and native students who are on scholarship will benefit from free room and board. The borders will get a monthly allowance whose amount is fixed by the high commissioner of the Republic.

Students for the Douala vocational school are recruited among students attending special classes in the territory. This competitive exam is different from the entrance examination for Douala superior primary school.

Candidates should be between the ages of thirteen and sixteen years.

11   High Commissioner
of the Cameroons
The Economic Kingdom

On August 27, 1940, when the mother country, then occupied and betrayed, was starting to live one of her darkest moments, the Cameroons did not despair of France; they heard General de Gaulle's call and joined Free France. All men from the Cameroons, whether European or African, were serving the same ideal, sharing a will to fight and drawing courage from the conviction that France could not perish because her cause was the very same one served by the Allied Nations in their battle for freedom against racism. They knew that the spiritual and physical resources of overseas France would be committed to the fullest in support of French patriots in their resistance struggle on the soil of the mother country.

Those who did not despair of France in 1940 are now witnessing her resurrection.

The Cameroons must participate in this resurrection as they did in the liberation of France. They must continue climbing the road to destiny as they did so marvellously on August 27, 1940. They will no longer carry arms and shed blood; they will now use machines and work along the road to freedom, equality, and brotherhood. Today, we are speaking of free men, equal in the eyes of law and brothers to one another.

Let us go to work! Our duty on the anniversary date of August 27, 1940, is to call everyone to work, to launch a crusade for work as the Cameroons on August 27, 1940, was called to launch a crusade for a Free

France and for liberation. Let unions, cooperatives, missions, all settlers and civil servants, all organizations and men who are supposed to serve as models take part in this task; let them organize the workers' army and proclaim holidays to celebrate work done with care and enthusiasm.

The future of the Cameroons does not lie in continuous feuding between different groups; it resides in rubber, coffee, cocoa, banana, palm, tobacco, and quinquina plantations; in the fields planted with peanuts and corn, in pastures and herds, in mines, in lumber sites, in sawmills, in the building of dams. Through the managing of all these partly developed and badly distributed riches, men from Africa will find happiness. The future of the Cameroons depends on better railway systems, on tar-surfaced roads and permanent bridges, on the port of Douala equipped for large trading operations and on an airport which already allows us to get to Paris in twenty hours. The future of the Cameroons rests in low-cost housing developments, schools, in the soon to be built university campus and in medical training.

Let us start working on the infrastructure of the Cameroons, which is indissolubly linked to social progress!

12   High Commissioner
of the Cameroons
The Political Kingdom: I

For the first time in the history of the Cameroons a representative assembly meets today, April 30, 1946. In the name of the Republic and of the minister of Overseas France, Marius Moutet, I bring you greetings, and thus I greet all the populations and activities represented by you. I am also happy to greet you individually, you who have been selected by electoral colleges or trusting colleagues to sit here in Douala.

Gentlemen, if there were people who had doubts about France, I would ask them to judge her generous act of today, which is only one among the many which marks its long history. When our country, recuperating after years of war, invasion, and ruin, would be considered entitled to look solely after herself, she fiercely goes on with her noble program of African emancipation. She reasserts her faith in Africa's human values and in her associates, the blacks and whites, Europeans and Africans of the French Union, in the management of our permanent, common interests. On this solemn day of your first session, I do not have to ask you to join the commissioner of the Republic in expressing our filial devotion toward France.

The principle that human nature is identical in substance in all races and in all places is one in which I very strongly believe and which I am entrusted to apply. This is the republican rule; it proceeds directly from our national tradition and Christian civilization. It is opposed to all forms of racism, whatever their source. When we apply this rule, it means that men of all races enjoy the same rights as well as the same obligations. Gentlemen, I invite you and your constituencies to mobilize all forces in order to make sure that blacks and whites have access to modern technology and to greater social justice. Let us be realistic and state that, in today's world situation, nothing will be accomplished in the Cameroons without the unity of blacks and whites. Nothing could be more normal to a Frenchman than this union. I emphatically affirm that nothing, nothing at all, can join men better than to gather them to accomplish a vast task which is important to all of them.

Freedom to work and the abolition of forced labor are not incompatible with volunteer work* and the exercise of fair authority. However, I ask you, Gentlemen, to make sure that your constituencies fully realize that if freedom to work is taken to mean laziness, the fate of the Cameroons is in jeopardy. All vagabonds are guilty of sabotage. A secretary of state who cannot be suspected of collusion with the possessing classes was recently telling the miners of Northern France: "To work is to be free." †

Of course planning is necessary. We have to set up a plan for acquiring the technical equipment which the Cameroons so desperately lacks. In order to wage a modern economic war, we need means other than the feeble arms of a population scattered over a large territory, decimated by disease and malnutrition. In order to score a victory against social evils, we need machines, not only bare chests.

We should also remember that, in a country almost as large as France but with only 2,800,000 inhabitants, if we try to be everywhere, we will accomplish nothing worthwhile anywhere. Of course, we do not want to give our efforts to some selected towns and in these towns to the European districts. On the contrary, it is a matter of developing whole regions; but we have to be careful about choosing the regions we want to work in first, because they will be models for the others. Let us start at the beginning: the port the only port for the Cameroons at present; then the railway system, which already exists but which has worn out equipment and is poorly laid out; roads that are already open but that cannot be properly kept up each year by men and shovels alone. These form the infrastructure which should be implanted immediately if we want to proceed in a coherent manner, develop key regions, and reach into the heart of the villages of the Cameroons.

*Fearing that the abolition of forced labor would lead to the neglect of important public works, some officials hoped that the appeal to voluntary labor would help accomplish these tasks (ed.).

†Maurice Thorez, secretary-general of the French Communist Party (ed.).

Gentlemen, I would like to conclude with one last point. You all realize that we are at a turning point in the evolution of the Cameroons; or, rather, that the Cameroons are now part of a worldwide evolution. Since the great wars, dramatic signs of an important revolution—new ideas and forces—are emerging which force us to revise our old conceptions of life and to search for novel means of action.

Politically, the old paternalistic organization which was an outgrowth of historical necessity must be replaced by a new organization based on collaboration with assemblies which will be similar to this one. This does not mean that governmental authority will become obsolete; on the contrary, such authority will be needed more than ever.

Economically, scattered pioneers can no longer be the rule. A Cameroons of unions and cooperatives is being born. Work and discipline will be more necessary than ever. If not, there will be no credit, no machines, and poverty for all. Now, then, let us look at reality. We have a hard but noble battle to fight. But, remember, our men are as good as any others. And when I say "Our men," I mean not only whites, civil servants, officers, planters, tradesmen, missionaries but also blacks, all blacks who live in all parts of this beautiful country.

13   High Commissioner
of the Cameroons
The Political Kingdom: II

1946 will have seen many elections.

There was in the first place the election of your own Assembly. Next, the referendum on the constitution. Then new elections for the National Assembly took place, followed by the referendum which approved the constitution of the Republic and the French Union. Finally parliamentary elections for the National Assembly were held, and tomorrow there will be elections for the new representative assembly of the Cameroons. If I am correct, there have been five elections so far and by the end of the year there will have been six.

These elections, very new in themselves and unusually frequent, had to be carried out under often difficult material circumstances. You had to face difficulties which the mother country, infinitely better trained and equipped, could hardly imagine at times. The fact that these elections took place in an orderly and dignified fashion is the more remarkable.

The electoral bodies made up according to the law, entered the life of the Cameroons and freely expressed their opinions. Three deputies, Messrs. Aujoulat, Douala Manga Bell, and Ninire now represent the Cameroons in the National Assembly of the Republic. All of them are very aware of the needs of the country to which they belong, either by birth or as a result of a long stay.

I shall not comment on the personalities of the elected officials. But I think I may be allowed to note that, in the recently emerging parliamentary life in the Cameroons, dissenting opinions allowed ideas and forces to confront one another naturally and freely within the framework of the law and that this marked an unprecedented occurrence in the country's history.

Hardly twenty-five years have elapsed since French trusteeship was established in the Cameroons. And now the Cameroons sends its representatives to the National Assembly in Paris and elects its own representative assembly. This is indeed very significant: it symbolizes the country's political evolution.

Important reforms have been formulated this year. They have been carried out without trouble, accepted by everybody. It is impossible to go back in time to disciplinary justice,* forced labor, and conscription.

The abolition of disciplinary justice, forced labor, and porterage is taking place smoothly and has already had the effect of bringing back home some 10,000 emigrants.

Employers' and workers' delegates are getting to know how labor law and collective bargaining work.

Salaries of civil servants have been raised twice, within the budgetary limits, by the administration negotiating with labor unions.

I hope that private firms, labor unions, and government will search together for solutions suitable to these difficult times in which we have to live and work.

In spite of the fact that this year required attention to be paid to many matters concerning events occurring both in the mother country and in the rest of the world, the French high commission, acting as trustee, fulfilled its mission and submitted here, in full agreement with your permanent commission, economic and social programs which will shape the future.

Now you are responsible for carrying out the program that has already been approved by your permanent commission.

Our mission is to overcome the difficulties of the postwar era, to assert our confidence in the future of the French Union and the Cameroons.

Mister President, Representatives, I declare open the second session of your assembly, the agenda of which is familiar to you. I am confident that I express your own feelings when I declare: Long live the Republic and the French Union! Long live the Cameroons!

*The indigénat (ed.).

14 High Commissioner
of the Cameroons
The Settlers

In the colonies, settler society has an importance which should neither be overemphasized nor treated as if it did not exist. The European population, whether civil servants, traders, or planters, forms a numerical minority but a minority holding key posts.

The Cameroons, when it was cut off from France, had strengthened its colonial characteristics. No one checked on its civil servants. Some of them, as well as settlers, had been to South Africa and had come back imbued with racist attitudes. In the Cameroons of Free France, some had even talked about establishing corporal punishment in order to strengthen the disciplinary nature of the native code and to force native workers to participate in "the war effort." The settlers in the Free Cameroons, more than in any other settler community, reinforced its attitudes as a closed society.

The Cameroons' first representative assembly, elected on April 7, 1946, was also the first one of its kind in French Black Africa. Since the assembly was elected by two different electoral colleges [a European and an African one], was it not natural that its two sections should deliberate separately? This hidden segregation was present in no text, but some hoped to establish it. For my part, I decided that the representative assembly would be one and only one and that its two sections would work together to represent a unified Cameroons and not a segregated one of blacks and whites.

15 High Commissioner
of the Cameroons
Some Doubts

Everything had to be built at once, from top to bottom. The requirement was to gather as best as possible and within the framework of brand new institutions all the diverse human elements of the Cameroons so that together they could build their own future.

We had to act in such a way that the United Nations' trusteeship over the Cameroons succeeded that of the League of Nations' mandate and that no obstacle at the local level hindered French diplomacy in elaborating agreements on trusteeship which undoubtedly would be discussed in New York at the end of 1946. At the same time, nothing was to be spared to make the Cameroons feel more and more integrated with France. This was possible since the Cameroons already took part in the working of our national institutions through its representatives, and since it was starting to take care of its own affairs thanks to the representative assembly that was born in the same year, 1946. The above tasks, which constituted my mission, could be viewed as contradictory only if we considered them separately. The mission could be carried out successfully if these objectives were combined to form, within a French whole, an original political entity that would neither be colonial nor dependent on a kind of international condominium but that would find in itself the resources for its development.

In 1946 the Cameroons, were made up of peasants and shepherds. What power could 16,000 voters out of a population of 3,200,000 exert? What means would the Cameroons' representatives be able to use to picture the aspirations of their constituencies to the different French assemblies? Finally, how strong would the Cameroons' representative assembly of thirty-four, then later forty, members, be in the face of the deep-rooted bureaucracy found in the administrative centers and in the bush posts? Was it not normal to fear that the realities of the Cameroons would be as incommunicable to people in the rostrum or halls of the assemblies as in the cumbersome bureaucracy?

As colonial administrators in direct contact with the bush and its shepherds and peasants, our usefulness was on the verge of disappearing because the new institutions would not leave room for people like us any more. The essential contribution we could make to the country—a modern, honest administration and an opportunity to build something greater than a village or a tribe—would not this contribution be endangered? On the other hand, the worst we could bring them— bureaucracy, routine, passivity—would survive and maybe bring disease to these budding institutions before they could even develop and bear fruit.

There is no doubt that we had a trusteeship duty toward the Africans. This was far from being easy; it was in fact very complex! Our task was to remain watchful and to make sure everyone understood this duty and this complexity.

While on my rounds, across these beautiful and varied regions which together would echo the heart of Africa, I would reflect upon the special quality of the times we lived in and the mission which all of us carried out—we the administrators, the civil servants of all ranks, the settlers of all types, and the still voiceless populations.

Sources

1. "L'Union française et le problème constitutionnel," *Politique* 1 (November 15, 1945): 412, 415–20, 426–27.

2. "Le Procès de la colonisation française," *Renaissances* 15 (October 25, 1945): 18–21.

3. "L'Union française—à l'échelle du monde, à la mesure de l'homme," *Esprit* 13 (July 1945): 231–33, 235.

4. "Lord Lugard et la politique africaine," *Africa* 21 (July 1951): 184–86.

5. "La République française et la communauté," in Marc Blancpain et al., *La France d'aujourd'hui* (Paris: A. Hatier, 1961), pp. 70–74, 79.

6. "L'Evolution de la politique des puissances coloniales après 1945," *Revue économique et sociale* (September 1960): 11–21.

7. *L'Afrique noire française et son destin*, pp. 18–23.

8. Ibid., pp. 70–71.

9. Decree, August 29, 1946, *Journal officiel du Cameroun français* (September 1, 1946): 1024–25.

10. Decree, April 27, 1946, *Journal officiel du Cameroun français* (May 15, 1946): 644–45.

11. Speech, August 27, 1946, *Journal officiel du Cameroun français* (September 1, 1946): 1009–10.

12. Speech, April 30, 1946, *Journal officiel du Cameroun français* (May 15, 1946): 617–20.

13. Speech, November 30, 1946, *Journal officiel du Cameroun français* (December 15, 1946): 1397–1400.

14. "Memoirs," chap. 2, "Une vie politique nouvelle," pp. 25–32, manuscript. Delavignette Papers, Archives nationales, section outre-mer, Paris.

15. Ibid., pp. 35–37.

5

Colonial Wars

The decolonization of the French empire was by no means a peaceful process. France's Asian empire, Indochina, was surrendered only after an eight-year-long war, Algeria after an equally long struggle.

As director of political affairs for the Ministry of Overseas France, Delavignette was responsible for giving advice to the minister on Indochinese affairs. A man not acquainted with the Orient, Delavignette relied on his instinct and his personal contacts with French officials in Indochina to evaluate French policy.

The French position in Indochina had suffered an eclipse as a result of the Japanese occupation in 1940. And even after the Second World War had ended, the French were never able to reestablish their control. Leading the nationalist movement in Vietnam was the Communist Ho Chi Minh, who declared the independence of Vietnam in September 1945. France recognized the independence the following March, but the recognition was ambiguous for it accepted Vietnamese independence within the framework of the Indochinese Union and the French Union, both of which were Paris-controlled. It was therefore inevitable that fighting between Ho Chi Minh's followers, the Viet Minh, and the French forces would break out. The latter included a large number of colonial troops, many of whom were Indochinese. Officially the French view was that its role was to see to it that a free and independent state, but one associated with France, be allowed to develop in Vietnam.

In one of the earliest memoranda we have, which Delavignette wrote to his minister, it is clear that he as yet saw the situation from a relatively optimistic viewpoint. While noting the precariousness of the French situation in 1948 in Vietnam, he was nevertheless hopeful that through better coordination of the various agencies in charge of the war effort success could come (1).

A few months later, however, Delavignette quite cogently argued that the war was a truly nationalist one which had parallels with the fight the French Resistance had waged against the Germans (2).

The French government, encouraged by officials in the field, decided in March 1949 to recognize the independence of Vietnam under the former emperor, Bao Dai. The so-called "Bao Dai solution" would presumably answer the Vietnamese demand for independence, win over the Vietnamese people against Ho, and still preserve the area within the French Union. Delavignette, however, was less than convinced that the Bao Dai solution was a workable one, and in a thoughtful memorandum in October 1949 expressed his reservations. He was to prove correct; Bao Dai was ineffective and was viewed by most Vietnamese as a French puppet. In the same memorandum, expressing misgiving about the Bao Dai solution, Delavignette spoke also of the geopolitical realities of the war and asked how long would it be possible for France to continue the struggle (3).

In the spring of 1950, with no foreseeable change in the Indochina war, Delavignette reiterated his apprehensions about the situation. He asked his minister to ponder whether the continued involvement in Indochina would not affect the rest of the French empire. To appease the demand for independence in Indochina, the French insisted that those overseas areas known as "associated territories" (most of them were in Indochina), although part of the French Union, were in fact either independent or virtually so. While such assertions might have to be made to preserve the "associated territories" within the French Union, would they not have an effect on the other territories that were part of the French Union, leading them also to desire independence? And a second consideration was raised. Would the Americans who were underwriting much of the French war and also helping to finance French reconstruction after World War II use their power to force France to curtail its influence over its African overseas territories? Specifically the Point Four Program was singled out as being a threat to France's black empire. President Truman in his 1949 inaugural address suggested as his "fourth point" that underdeveloped countries be given American aid. Could France's territories advance economically only at the price of loosening ties with the mother country? (4)

Even after retiring from the Ministry of Overseas France in 1951, Delavignette continued to play a role in overseas affairs. As a member of the Conseil économique, a governmental advisory body, he did not shirk the opportunity in 1955 to explain to the government the social and economic origins of the war in Algeria. The war had broken out in 1954 and was not viewed by French officialdom as a legitimate nationalist uprising but rather as the work of some misguided lawbreakers. In a long, detailed report, some of which is here excerpted, Delavignette pointed out the social and economic matrix of the rebellion. Somewhat unrealistically, he seemed to believe that if the past inequities were taken care of Algeria could still be won over to the French cause (5).

The scandal of the French use of torture and of other inhumane actions by the French in Algeria became publicly known in 1957, and under public prodding the government appointed a Commission for the Safeguard of Human Rights in Algeria. Delavignette was one of its prominent members, and he went to Algeria and reported in detail the violations he discovered. He soon concluded, however, that the commission had been named to shield the government from further criticisms and that it had no real intention of stopping the criticized practices in the future. Thus, shortly after filing his report, he resigned (6). Retrospectively viewing the Algerian war, Delavignette explained how torture in Algeria affected the moral health of Frenchmen and how the French experience revealed the capacity for evil inherent in every society. The deceit which accompanied the war, Delavignette stated, had left an open wound in France's conscience (7).

In French colonial thought, Algeria was always viewed as the linchpin between France and her black colonies. The failure to create a just and peaceful society in Algeria, Delavignette at one point remarks, may have been what cost France her black African territories. If Algeria had been preserved, so could have the rest of the African territories (8).

1 Indochina
The Solution—Better French
Coordination of the War Effort

We are not trying to reconquer Indochina; we just want to protect populations that still need our help and to give them a hand in establishing the Associated State of Vietnam that they hope for. But, of course, such a policy should be carried out in a consistent fashion.

It is becoming more and more apparent that our army, which numbers over 100,000 men, can hardly keep a few centers secure. The Indochinese tragedy is stopping or hindering the harmonious development of the French Union and weighs on our international position as well as on our domestic policy.

What caused our failures?

On the whole, we tend to throw the responsibility on our Vietnamese partners. The nationalists who join us allegedly are all mediocre men; all talented people supposedly have espoused the Viet Minh cause.

Other observers believe we are the victims of a combination of circumstances in Asia. Asian populations are stirred up by an irresistible wave of nationalism which makes the continuing political control by

Europe over them impossible. If these propositions are true, then the solutions posed are too simplistic.

We have to look for the primary cause of our failures in the lack of unity present in our politico-military leadership.

Everyone knows the Indochina question cannot be solved militarily. It requires that political moves be taken in close conjunction with military actions. But this liaison is presently not a satisfactory one.*

2   Indochina
Some Disturbing Parallels

We must take into account this fiery young nationalism which the Viet Minh have developed and spread. We do not have unconditional followers anymore. And those we still have set conditions; the first one is removal of our colonial control of Cochin China.† Even our followers are not without some feeling of the muffled hatred which is building up against us. We can see, in the hateful atmosphere, a gaping wound, which poisons all our actions in the country. However painful to us a comparison between the Viet Minh and our Resistance under German occupation might be, we should realize that it is a comparison frequently heard among Vietnamese intellectuals. We are taken for an occupying force with which one should not compromise and against which any means is justified, even that of the Viet Minh. And to the masses, the Viet Minh do not represent communism but, first of all, independence and also an authority which is already being felt.

With the exception of the Mois plateaus, we are holding only towns and a few regions outside of which the guerrilla forces reappear after we are gone. Our military posts are hopelessly surrounded, unable to break their encirclement and to become a constructive force.

Army morale suffers from the feeling that our means are qualitatively and quantitatively inadequate and our goals unclear. Here is an excerpt from a letter from a French official in Indochina: "Every high officer performs his glorious deed in order to be promoted. After each glorious deed, the officer gratified by the state flees swiftly and leaves to his succeeding colleague a tragic situation to handle."

Have I painted a bleak picture? It is up to the appropriate official to

*There follows a series of proposals for administrative reorganization in Paris to permit closer coordination of political and military policy toward Indochina (ed.).

†Shortly after the French had recognized the independence of Vietnam, they had tried to limit Ho Chi Minh's authority by subtracting the southern part, Cochin China, and declaring it still to be a direct dependency of France (ed.).

put things in their proper light when he shortly gives you a report on the development of the situation.*

But I had to reveal my thoughts to you . . . .

3 Indochina
Can the War be Won?

The principle of our "Bao Dai policy" depends upon the value attributed to the tradition of the Annamite monarchy as incarnated by Bao Dai.

Around the tradition thus personified it has been suggested that the Vietnamese nationalists might be rallied away from the Viet Minh. It would then be possible to pacify the country with the help of a Vietnamese army, which would have to be created, and to lay the foundation for a modern Vietnam, an associated state within the French Union. All things considered, Bao Dai seems to be the only man who could face Ho Chi Minh, but is he really "the worthy leader and the capable man"† he is described to be?

The internal logic of the policy he has to carry out requires him to become emperor again. But is not such a policy counter to the movement which is stirring up South-East Asia in general and Vietnam in particular?

I do not reject the value of the March 8 agreement, which ratifies the Bao Dai policy. But neither do I want us to forget the distance between this agreement and the true situation in Vietnam.

We are dealing with an impoverished country in a state of war. Half the railway system is destroyed; the number of users is not even a sixth of what it was in 1938. Peasants are paying taxes twice: to the French administration and to Ho Chi Minh. They long for peace and security. But can we give them what they want with the means now at our disposal? Military operations and institutions are not enough. *A strong local administration is needed.*

Thus Bao Dai has to be "the worthy leader and the capable man" in order to build immediately the *basic organization* on which our Vietnamese policy would rest. That is his task. Yes, he may have ministers and diplomats but if he does not have, above all, competent administrators, in touch with the country at large, capable of heading the different local agencies, he will not be tuned in to the facts of Vietnam's life nor will we.

*Many of the higher officials serving in Indochina sent optimistic reports on the situation there to Paris. One of these officials was returning to Paris at the time when Delavignette wrote this note; he seems to have regarded these men with skepticism (ed.)

†An expression used frequently by the French supporters of Bao Dai (ed.).

French public opinion is increasingly reticent regarding the Indochinese question. The heavy death toll suffered by expeditionary forces—17,000 men from 1945 to 49*—has brought mourning to many French towns and villages; the hundreds of billions of francs eaten up by the Indochinese war—150 billion are anticipated for 1950†—seem to pay for only illusory policies. The public is unnerved by all these bloody battles that bring no quick and decisive solutions on either the political or military front. And some political parties as well as some important persons feel that the Indochinese cause is bad in that it is giving France a guilty conscience.

Are not the efforts required from France by the Vietnamese situation beyond our means? Is the relief of the expeditionary corps by soldiers from France adequate? Will our depleted finances be able to carry on this war for long?

If these questions had been asked at a time when Asia was still quiet, was not stirred up by communism, we might have thought that a solution existed to all the Franco-Vietnamese problems. But such is not the case anymore.

We cannot ignore the increasing dangers: dangers faced by a 138,000-man expeditionary force fighting 12,000 kilometers from its French bases; dangers faced by French civil servants and settlers; and dangers faced by those Vietnamese who have courageously embraced our cause.

I am not trying to be overly dramatic. Rather it is my duty to reveal my thoughts to you on the matter, and I want to keep you informed.

4   Indochina
Vietnam—At What Cost?

The Vietnamese government received the powers that we gave to it, according to the March 8, 1949, agreements. The government established a ministerial and diplomatic superstructure which allows it to keep up appearances or delusions. But it has no social infrastructure in its own country.

Bao Dai has worn out his enemies but not his true enemy, Ho Chi Minh.

The people undoubtedly want peace, and surely the Viet Minh are only an active minority. But why is Bao Dai, "the worthy leader and the capable man," according to an official report, taking his time in forming another active minority which the masses could trust and which could counterbalance the Viet Minh?

I should add that the Indochina war is more and more unpopular.

*We all know that the Riff war cost only 3,500 lives [Delavignette's note].
†This was $300 million at the then existing exchange rate (ed.).

Instead of being one of those great national and human causes which
France embraces totally, it appears to be at times a moral tragedy which
divides France and, at other times, an incident in the Cold War which
reaches beyond France.

Vietnam in Relationship to
Our Overseas Territories

It usually is said that the different parts of the French Union are bound
together and that all of them should, whatever the cost, remain so that
the union does not crumble away.

A disaster in Vietnam obviously would have repercussions on all our
African territories. I believe that these repercussions would be even
greater for the mother country. We should avoid a situation in which we
shall suffer a disaster in Vietnam.

You are in charge of our policy that consists of integrating the African
territories into the Republic, a policy of integration which is that much
more necessary because elsewhere we have to put the emphasis on the
independence of the Associated States.

Don't you think that your policy of integration might be altered by
the Indochina War? I am not alluding to the financial aspect of it; I do
not emphasize the fact that an extra battalion in Indochina represents
fewer schools, hospitals, and roads for Africa and that, with the 150
billion francs which we have been spending yearly for five years on the
Indochina War, we could have built a prosperous and strong Africa.

Another danger to our situation in Africa is that the U.S.A., as a trade-
off against her aid in Indochina, might force us, through the Point Four
Program, to accept that our African territories cease being integrated.
What would our position be then?* We would have endangered the
future of French Africa, and for what gain in the Far East? For keeping
alive the influence of the West at the cost of a dirty war in which France
plays the role of the "ugly white man."

Is it not in the U.S.A.'s interest that we become more involved in the
Asian war while they intervene in Africa by means of economic
investments which will lead to political control? In such a situation,
should we not foresee that we shall be forced to choose between the
necessity of either continuing our war effort in Asia or relinquishing our

---

*Delavignette evidently feared that the Americans would use the Point Four
Program (the offer of American technical aid to underdeveloped regions of the
world), as a lever to force the French to loosen their ties with Africa. Such fears
were common among French colonial officials, who had experienced Franklin
Roosevelt's anticolonialism and in Indochina had found that Americans, in
exchange for their military aid, were increasingly pressuring for liberalization of
French control in the Asian possession (ed.).

freedom of action in Africa? I firmly believe that it is our African interests which, in the last analysis, should take precedence over any other consideration. France's future is in Africa with the Africans.

In short:

a) Is the time right to try to win over the Viet Minh's noncommunist, nationalist elements?

b) Is Bao Dai the worthy leader and the man capable of building a Vietnam united with the French Union?

c) Will the American help in Indochina require a more or less hidden compensation in Africa?

d) Must we tie Africa's fate to the risk we are taking in Vietnam? These are the questions which the situation forces us to consider.

5 Algeria
Report on the Social and Economic Situation

Algeria's accelerated population increase is its most important problem and dominates all social and economic issues. Algeria, which represents less than 3/1000 of the world population, is growing at a yearly rate of 1% of the world increase.

From 1872 to 1918, in three-quarters of a century, the population grew three and a half times. And this already high rate has been accelerating during the past few years. A study showed that the population increased by 240,000 within the year 1952. This increase corresponds to a demographic progression rate of 2.5%, one of the highest in the world. According to the last census, taken in 1954, Algeria had 9,531,000 people (workers in foreign countries included), of which 1,230,000 were European.

It is the Moslem population which has undergone considerable increase; it increased almost fourfold in a century, from 2,300,000 in 1856 to 8,232,000 in 1953. The birthrate is very high—320,000 Moslem babies are born every year—and consequently the Moslem population is young. More than half the population is not 20 years of age: (3,279,000 adults for 3,502,000 children aged 1 to 14), or 94 adults for 100 children.

In contrast to the growing expenses faced by the community (because of this growing Moslem population), agricultural production has been approximately the same since prewar times, and industrial production is increasing only slightly.

One of the social consequences of this population pressure, with no production increase to balance it, is a population move from the rural regions to the cities, where unemployment and underemployment have been on the rise since the end of the war.

Characteristics of
Unemployment in Algeria

Unemployment in the mother country is linked to the economy and is thus cyclical and temporary. In Algeria, by contrast, unemployment and underemployment are due to an underdeveloped economy and an increasing population; consequently they are permanent. The Algerian economy, even during a favorable phase, cannot absorb in its present structure the surplus of working population which a constantly increasing population brings to the job market. Everyone is aware that the Algerian economic potential, which was seemingly adequate to its population needs before the war, is now quite incapable of compensating for the demographic situation, even in normal years. An important characteristic of the Algerian job market lies in the fact that it is the rural population which is most affected; there, figures indicate a catastrophic situation.

Last, it should be emphasized that unemployment and underemployment affect the Moslem population only and that the 1,200,000 Algerians of French extraction escape the situation entirely.

Thus, all efforts should be directed toward maximum economic development.

If we want to solve the problem of unemployment and underemployment, all investments should be aimed at creating a more complete integration of the Moslem population into the Algerian economy.

We remind ourselves that the preamble of the Constitution stipulates that everyone has a right to a job. Furthermore, article 81 asserts that "all Frenchmen and French Union nationals possess the status of citizen of the French Union; a status which grants them the rights and freedoms guaranteed in the preamble of the present Constitution." It is useless to argue about the gap which exists between principles and realities. The Constitution must be observed by all and especially by the public powers, if we do not want the French state to weaken.

[The difference between European and Moslem employment is also reflected in the food consumption of the two groups.] In their *Economie alimentaire du globe*, Cépède and Lengelli give us the following figures for the Algerian standard of living, translated into calories: 1,802 per day as opposed to 2,979 for France herself. Algeria is thus nutritionally deprived vis à vis the mother country. In Algeria itself we find a similar imbalance among its different populations.

We will not dwell on the danger that such a situation represents for Algeria and France.

We must elaborate a food plan which is balanced nutritionally as well as economically. Our goal is a victory over shortages and malnutrition.

Education

Today only 436,577 children out of a school-age population of 2 million go to school.

Such a situation requires a massive financial effort to remedy. Only sixteen percent of the Algerian budget is allocated to education.

Land Policy

In Algeria, lands are divided into two important categories: lands which are called Frenchified because they fall under French law (5,800,000 hectares) and lands which are under common law (about 5,600,000 hectares).

Some estates now are latifundia which are either insufficiently developed or whose special needs are neglected. These estates are sometimes rented, at high prices, to a multitude of small fellahs.

It is conceivable that it would be timely to buy these estates back, divide them into small plots, and sell them to those who cultivate them. Long-term loans should be available to peasants to allow them to become landowners without having to face the insuperable difficulty of having no money.

Industrialization

Algerian industrialization would allow a superabundant manpower to find jobs; at the same time it would raise the standard of living through the creation of wealth. It is by implementing a program of industrialization that overpopulated and underdeveloped countries are trying to solve the dual problem of providing employment and raising the standard of living.

General Conclusions

Let us try now to draw some general conclusions from this report.

While we want to remain aloof from political considerations which are outside our jurisdiction, we cannot ignore that very serious events are taking place as this document is being elaborated and submitted. Without stretching our role, without going beyond the tasks given to our assembly, it is our duty to declare that the present situation is the partial result of the social and economic imbalance previously analyzed and that it will not be rectified if this imbalance continues to exist.

When land is lacking, when workers are out of work, when youth has no hope, then public authority is no more than an empty shell.

The measures we advocate in the enclosed blueprint come from two broad, related concepts.

The first states that fast and sure action is required in both the social and economic spheres. Industrialization is a very important task, and no Algerian future can be erected without it. Let us create immediately the necessary conditions: let us research what kind of industries should be implanted and study their potential outlets in the Algerian and foreign markets; let us discover how to lure investments, how to fight dumping, and also offer professional training for workers and technicians. None of these measures can be neglected without dangerous consequences, nor can they be merely improvised.

Second, whether we are dealing with agriculture or industrialization or, more exactly, with the two, and however important Algerian financial self-help may be, it is up to France herself to come up with most of the financing.

The subventions and loans that will launch Algerian economic and social progress will have to be lured, for the most part, from the mother country's national revenue and, as a last resort, through direct and indirect taxation.

More than ever, Algeria, as well as the overseas territories, needs a government which has a feel for human problems and a talent for human relationships. The administrative personnel must know Algeria in depth, especially in dealing with the psycho-sociological implementation of the economic plan. Just as one cannot conceive of a rural cooperative and an office for rural progress without Arab-speaking personnel, one cannot imagine a plan without personnel capable of working for it, of adapting it if need be, of translating and explaining it to everyone. Why could not this task be given to Moslems, who could be trained quickly to help with the psychological aspects of the plan's implementation? Their participation might guarantee the success of the plan by involving the population. And the French government would, for its part, be able to check the plan against local realities and make changes during implementation. To accomplish this the science of man must be brought into this great project. The plan must be innovative in both the social and economic fields. Otherwise, the credits granted by the mother country will not be used to the fullest.

6 Algeria
Torture and Murder

During my stay in Algeria, whether in Algiers or Oran, I always kept in mind two facts that I should present at the beginning of this report. The first one is that the dominant characteristic of the situation in these two cities is that of a war situation. A very special war but a war nevertheless. The second fact is the atrociousness with which terrorism is carried out by our enemies. The internal logic of this special war affects, as we will see, our own behavior. Algiers' 900,000 inhabitants and

Oran's 300,000 apparently lead a normal life. We hardly notice a few precautionary measures by the army and police, to which we quickly get accustomed. Take the bus in Algiers: two armed guards will ask you not to stand on the platform where they keep guard. Visit Oran: a few yards away from streets which are as lively as those in any southern French city, you discover barbed wire, which obstructs the path leading to a "native" section of town.

Everywhere we sense that war hangs over and infiltrates daily life. The local newspapers will declare on one page that Algeria is not in the midst of a fiery war, as is said in the mother country, and will announce on the same page that funeral services will be held for Mr. X or Y who was cowardly murdered by "rebels," and that children wounded by a terrorist had to be hospitalized.

We witness two intermingling situations: a war situation which has nothing to do with classical warfare and normal activity which is not quite that found in time of peace. This continual oscillation between war and peace affects the psyche of individuals as well as whole communities. Sometimes people go about their peacetime activities, sometimes they are caught by war necessities. They go to work, do their jobs, trying to forget that the children they left at home can be blown up by a terrorist explosion. They fear the pressure of being torn between the opposing forces of war and peace. Such is the climate in which people live here.

The Ain-Isser (District of Tlemcen)
and Mercier-Lacombe (District
of Mascara) Affairs

On July 11, the day after I arrived in Algiers, I visited General Salan, commander in chief in Algeria, and talked to him about these two affairs which had been brought to my attention in Paris and which were one of my chief reasons for coming here.

General Salan immediately gave me the succinct reports he had in his possession and which I describe below. He told me that the complete files were in Oran, in the hands of the Office of Military Justice, and that I could consult them there.

First, the report concerning the Ain-Isser affair. On the night of March 13, 1957, the 12th company of the 7th Infantry Regiment, under Lieutenant Curutchet's command, detained thirty-three suspects caught during an operation. Since their identities were supposed to be checked only the following day, the suspects were confined in an unused wine storehouse in which were stored empty vats not used since 1942; the measurements of the vats are 3 meters x 3.50 meters x 3 meters, the air capacity about 30 cubic meters. A hole at the base allowed a man to enter, and fresh air entered through a hole at the top. The following day, March 14, the thirty-three suspects were taken out of their makeshift jail. All were perfectly healthy.

On the night of March 14, the 12th company detained 101 more suspects. The same solution was used. Each container received twenty-five Algerian French Moslems (FMA) except one, which received twenty-six. The following day, seventeen corpses were found in one wine container, twenty-four in another one. The surviving men in these two containers claimed to have made noise during the night in order to alert their guards, but they had not been heard. It was later discovered that while the two vats containing the corpses externally appeared to be the same size as the others, they were smaller inside.

On the afternoon of the fifteenth, Lieutenant Curutchet told the battalion officer what had happened and asked him for two trucks to escort men who would dispose of the corpses.

On March 16, the corpses were scattered in a forbidden zone at about fifty kilometers from Ain-Isser. The advantage of this was that, in case the corpses should be discovered, they could easily be attributed to the FLN. They were not buried, just hidden in the bushes.

Fearful of the consequences, the officers informed their superiors.

The result: the general in command of the army corps in Oran entrusted the judicial inquiry to a Tlemcen police officer.

Disciplinary measures: Lieutenant Curutchet—thirty days arrest, suspended from command. Battalion Chief Castet-Barou—thirty days incarceration.

Judiciary measures: a charge of involuntary manslaughter was drawn up on April 5 against Lieutenant Curutchet and Second Lieutenant Closse.

Mercier Lacombe [Affair]

Here is the report concerning the second affair.

During an operation conducted at Ain-Touila, two men from the CCAS [Campagnie de commandement d'administration et des services] of the 1/219th Infantry Regiment were wounded. Convinced that the local population gave shelter to rebels, a police operation was conducted there, and twenty-three suspects were arrested and entrusted to the guard of the CCAS of the 1/219th infantry regiment. The suspects, reluctant to cooperate, were confined in a wine cellar on orders from Second Lieutenant Lefebvre, a battalion intelligence officer. At 3 A.M. the officer on duty reported nothing abnormal. On the morning of April 17, the death of the twenty-three suspects due to suffocation from an emanation of $SO_{2{12}}$, was reported.

Disciplinary measure: both officers were given a sentence of fifteen days.

Judiciary measure: an indictment for involuntary manslaughter against Commandant Holl is sought.

There is no need to emphasize the gravity of these two affairs, and it is not up to me to pass judgment on the sentences given by the military court. But I think it is our commission's duty not only to place events like those of Ain-Isser and Mercier-Lacombe in their war context, but also to note the great youth of these inexperienced officers. We are fighting a very special kind of war which, as of now, has not yet been taught in military schools and which requires generals to grope for new strategic concepts in the field. And in this war, it is on the shoulders of inexperienced lieutenants and second lieutenants that the direction of an operation rests.

It is also our commission's duty to ask how twenty-three deaths could occur on April 16 in circumstances similar to those in which forty-one deaths had occurred only a month earlier and at a distance of only 120 kilometers?

Between these two days, what had those in authority done to warn officers of the necessity to avoid the recurrence of such a "mistake"? They merely sent a memo dated April 18, which in very general terms, without reference to the Ain-Isser affair, alluded only to "recent incidents."

Furthermore, I learned by accident, a day before my departure, that on June 27, twenty-one suspects died of suffocation in a wine vat. This incident proves, at the least, that orders are not followed or that they have not been formulated with strong, clear words.

Another important related aspect should be called to attention. It is the dissimulation in the disposition of the corpses in the Ain-Isser affair. It reveals a certain state of mind that can be understood only if we remember the climate and the situation which prevail here and to which I will often return.

Lieutenant Curutchet most probably panicked when he discovered that forty-one suspects had died because elementary safety rules were not followed; forty-one deaths in these circumstances represented indeed something much graver than an "incident," as the April 18 memo called it. The lieutenant tried to hide the corpses that would constitute the evidence. Who helped him to secure men and materials to carry out his funerary task? Who covered him morally in this operation? It is not up to me to direct the inquest and prosecution of these cases. Our commission is not supposed to meddle with the system of justice. Ain-Isser is very close to the commune of Lamoricière, but the civil authorities there did nothing. And I am also struck by the fact that the population did not react publicly. Only Agha Bouamedi, who had two relatives among the suspects, dared speak to the colonel. The population remained silent but was suffering from the shock of terror or from indifference. And the Europeans were indifferent or frightened. To protest? What is the use!

The guilty party was the system that provoked panic in a twenty-six-year-old lieutenant and locked up a whole people in silence—a silence only those who secretly came in touch with our Commission for the Safeguard of Human Rights in Paris were able to overcome.

Which system are we talking about? The one within which our own authorities are struggling for authority because no clear demarcation exists among them. One consequence of this state of affairs is that the Moslem population does not know whom to turn to anymore.

The Ain-Isser affair showed how much the Moslem population distrusted the French authorities of this region; these authorities seem also to be locked up in a system which is in the process of destroying everything.

Terrorism and Counterterrorism

I have come to the thorniest section of my report.

I do not want to omit speaking about terrorism, its atrocities, massacres, sadistic mutilations.

It lays a trap for us which is called counterterrorism. I mean by that a caricature of a fight against terrorism.

Counterterrorism expresses itself in two ways.

A. Under the guise of French patriotism, counterterrorist groups arrogate to themselves the right to exercise police and judicial powers against all those they perceive to be enemies. In Algiers, some heads of these groups play the role of informer and see a suspect in every Frenchman who does not follow a certain conformist behavior. Suspect is the Catholic who does not share the ideas of the 10th Green Beret division chaplain, Father Delarue, about "intense" questioning. Suspect is the university professor who believes that requisitioning of schools will hamper learning. Suspect is the Moslem who deplores that troops invaded a mosque and killed its imam. Suspect is the retired civil engineer who will be accused of being a slanderous informer because he denounced policemen who were robbing a defenseless Moslem in broad daylight. Suspect is the high official who declares: "Give me the means to form a normal and powerful police and I will get rid of the zealots who think they can impose on me their shady ways of operating."

In its second form, no less pernicious than the first, counterterrorism not only conducts operations parallel to those of the army and the government but infiltrates the army and the government. Under the guise of efficiency, it shows a complete lack of respect for human life. Too many "fugitives" are shot down while "collecting wood"; too many "missing persons" are reported after an intense "questioning." People are arrested without officials with special powers even being consulted and without regular agencies being notified. Men released by either civil or military courts are thrown back into prison upon leaving the court.

The military and civil personnel who let themselves be caught in the terrorist machine will go back to the mother country one day. Can we believe that their return will rid them of automatic reactions acquired in Algeria and that they will recover the principles which honor their regiment or their agency?

I wonder what could have caused such a deterioration.

There seems to me a determining factor: the absolute lack of coordination between the great civil agencies on the one hand and the heads of the army on the other. Let us not mince words: a hypocritical state of siege reigns in Algeria.* I do not have to know if a regular state of siege would be better, but I firmly declare that the hypocritical situation infects all relationships between civil and military personnel and widens the gap between Europeans and Arabs.

In conclusion, I can only say that it is time, high time, to correct the situation as a whole in Algeria. In fact very little time is left.

Because the SAS† is already established there and the army is successful, a miraculous change still can occur. But the confusion existing between the different powers must be eradicated, and the fight against terrorism must not be perverted by a system which drives 80 percent of the Arabs against us. These Arabs constitute most of the Arabo-Berber population which, despite so many past extortions and so many present tragedies, still keeps its trust in justice, in France, and in a new French Algeria.

7   Algeria
Gangrene

The Algerian war still poses the problem of torture in France. This important problem is analyzed with clarity by the historian Pierre Vidal-Naquet in his latest book, *La Torture dans la République*. The title of the book is very explicit; it indicates that torture cannot be limited to a specific area and that it goes beyond the military and police framework within which it was used and concealed.

*"Hypocritical siege" in the sense that the army had arrogated to itself full powers, thus abrogating the civil rights of all Algerians without proclaiming a legal state of siege (ed.).

†Sections Administratives Spécialisées. This local administrative branch, often manned by young Frenchmen, was thought capable cf winning the population back (ed.).

I am aware of the arguments used for its justification: "There is no other way to operate, especially in a subversive war. If you were in charge of law and order, wouldn't you resort to torture in order to get information which would prevent the massacre of innocent people by plastic bombs?" I also know the argument which is no more than sighing or crying, "All wars are dirty! It is useless to think that one can remain clean in such situations."

General de Bollardière never condoned or used torture in Algeria. In his interview with the newspaper *Ouest France*, dated February 21, 1972, he shows us how the problem of torture can be examined, beyond the scope of war.

Whatever our past or present position toward the Algerian war may be, we have to realize that the industrial society we live in is, with its inhuman rhythm of work, filled with aggression conducive to violence and propitious to a return of torture in scientific forms.

Cain is for all seasons, and dwells in each of us. So does Pontius Pilate, who forever stained his hands by having washed them. Should we give in to this? Will we let torture slyly find its place in repression, and later in the prevention of acts which obviously would qualify as subversive? This would in fact corrupt the state.

Ten years after the Algerian war, the problem of torture still concerns all of us; if we do not react against it, we will remain passive in the face of subversion. The Christian knows—how could he forget it at this time of year?—that the worst sin is the pride that refuses guilt and that lies in order to avoid confessing. I publicly resigned from the Commission for the Safeguard of Human Rights, not to play the role of the moralist above the crowd, but to avoid lying by omission in my duty as a commissioner.

Blood dries quickly, said General de Gaulle. Blood, yes, but not pus. In the wound of the Algerian war, deceit is pus.

8   Algeria: Key to Black Africa

If only we could have created in Algeria harmony between two communities so different in their origins, separated by religion but united by the common task they should have carried out. If this task had only been suggested, even after the 1954 rebellion, by means other than a massive and negative repression! If only boldness and creativity, instead of being used to violate the penal code and to outdo the FLN's atrocities, had been channeled into an agrarian reform and the destruction of privileges! Then, Algeria would have been the linchpin of a French Eurafrica. Alas! You torturers who so readily used electrodes on your victims!

Sources

1. "Note pour Monsieur le Ministre Paul Coste-Floret," July 17, 1948. Delavignette Archives, Archives nationales, section outre-mer, Paris.

2. "Note pour Monsieur le Ministre," February 22, 1949, Delavignette Archives.

3. "Indochine," October 29, 1949, Delavignette Archives.

4. "Note sur la situation au Viet-Nam," April 30, 1950, Delavignette Archives.

5. Conseil économique, *Journal officiel, République Française* (July 5, 1955), pp. 326–57.

6. "Rapport de mission en Algérie," July 21, 1957. Privately communicated to editor. This report has also been reprinted in Pierre Vidal-Naquet, ed., *La Raison d'état* (Paris, 1962), pp. 171–84.

7. "Le Pus dans la plaie," *La Croix* (March 30, 1972), p. 14.

8. *L'Afrique noire française et son destin*, p. 176.

6

The Colonial Legacy
The Present and
Future Role of France
in Africa

With the end of the colonial era, Delavignette put into perspective the contributions of French rule to the newly independent states. The first and most obvious contribution was that the boundaries of the states, formed by the imperial scramble, now become national frontiers (1). Delavignette saw the colonial heritage continued in the field of administration although he recognized in that continuation both positive and negative qualities. The formal structure of the administration was continued along with some of its negative features, such as the failure to win the total trust of the population. While discussing the continuities, Delavignette also discussed the contemporary problems of African administration, problems which a dozen years after their writing are still relevant to the African situation (2, 3).

Delavignette believed that a good understanding of the colonial past was necessary if a constructive relationship between France and her former territories was to be created. In his view many commentators in the former colonies and in France had unfairly painted the colonial experience in dark hues. Africans should remember the benefits which accrued to them from the colonial era, and the French should recognize that it was they who had wanted an empire. It was cowardly to turn one's back suddenly on the imperial past and blame colonial officials for the imperial interlude. Here Delavignette was reflecting the bitterness many colonial officials felt when suddenly, after nearly a century of colonialism, they were faced by anticolonial thought in France and abroad (4, 5, 6, 7).

One of the legacies France left her former colonies and which has motivated her continued concern overseas has been the use of the French language. In 1958, when the African territories were increasingly moving toward independence, Delavignette expressed the rationale for and his hope that the former territories would preserve the French language (8). The use of French overseas put cultural and moral obligations on France to see that the societies which spoke French were on the road to economic development and social justice, Delavignette wrote in 1967 (9).

The French have continued to exercise a kind of "neoimperialism" by their concern for maintaining and even spreading the use of their language. Delavignette reflected the main motive for France's continuing aid to her former possessions.

In French, foreign aid is called "cooperation"; such cooperation, Delavignette declared, was a two-way street. France could not impose her values overseas; she had to take into account the needs of the countries asking help. And she had to consider, as much as those who received the aid, what the funds would be expended for. Could economic progress abolish hunger and poverty without bringing overseas the worst features of the industrialized world? Delavignette reveals here a sensitive approach to the environment not frequently shown by his contemporaries (10).

As part of French technical assistance, young Frenchmen known as "cooperants" are sent overseas. In a page addressed to them Delavignette spoke of their duties and obligations in Africa (11).

After decolonization larger numbers of Frenchmen completely lost interest in the former colonial territories. Delavignette's writings since 1960, on the contrary, asserted that even if the formal bonds have been broken, there are continuing obligations of human solidarity that bind France to the poor and economically deprived regions of the globe. Historical experience and personal ties mean that France has a special obligation to her former possessions. Delavignette wrote several articles impelled by the drought of the late 1960s and early 1970s. An excerpt from one of these calls for aid to the drought areas (12). In his memoirs, Delavignette greeted the declaration of the town of Chauvigny in France as "twin city" of his beloved Banfora in Upper Volta as a symbolic tie that affirmed the universality of man and the obligations which the advanced industrial world has to the poorer regions (13).

1   Political Legacy

It has not been noted often enough that independence made good use of former colonial borders in Black Africa, especially in Central and West Africa. Mapped out in a very arbitrary fashion by the European powers which partitioned Africa among themselves, the borders remain unquestioned by the new emerging African states. They find their natural cradles in territories cut out by colonization because these territories were in effect given an identity ("Africanized") by the European bush administrators.

Contrary to what so many ill-informed people believe, colonization did not mean oppression of countries that failed to establish their national boundaries until they achieved their independence. Reality is very different: the African spirit has nationalized colonial territories that served as foundations for sovereign states.

2 Administrative Legacy: I

The African prefect has replaced the colonial commandant. But the question arises: what kind of a bureaucracy should he head? How can it work smoothly and remain in touch with the masses who do not live in the administrative towns? As I write, Africa is experiencing several military coups d'état; five years after independence, republics are ousting their presidents elected just a few months before by almost unanimous votes of the people. We can see that something vital to national life is missing and that communications between infrastructures and super-structure, between the base and the summit, do not exist. African governments face many problems, among which those related to the district should not be ignored. The district remains one area where law and order can best be enforced and where national unity can be forged.

Let us have a closer look at African bureaucracy. In the capitals, we can see the machinery of a modern state, as well as its pomp, in its agencies and, at the international level, its embassies. But is not the district lacking some of this machinery? We declare a country to be underadministered when a bureaucracy swells and fills the capital, while in the bush country the lack of civil servants hampers all efforts toward development. One of the most pernicious forms of this ailment (one not peculiar to Africa!) can be found in the language used by bureaucrats. This language, with special terminology for each branch, full of meaning-less words, is understood only by the initiated and not at all by the masses. Even if in independent Africa the district prefect is an African and not a colonial commandant, if he loses direct contact with the villages, if his rule seems to them embodied in obscure jargon, he will be guilty of underadministration.

Before criticizing Africa, however, one should always keep its limited means in mind. Average annual income is 40,000 francs CFA per inhabitant in the relatively prosperous states; income falls to 5,000* francs where nomadic shepherds live.

Let us limit ourselves to two important social problems—education

*40,000 francs was $160 at the then current exchange rate; 5,000 francs was $20 (ed.).

and health. Ideally, one schoolteacher is needed for every 100 inhabitants, and WHO* would make do with one doctor for 10,000 inhabitants, just to prevent the recurrence of deadly epidemics. How can each
district receive the number of schoolteachers and doctors it needs? This
task would be possible to achieve if carried out within the framework of
French-African cooperation in a world at peace. But, for a foundation,
active districts are required even if only to supervise programs of school
attendance and vaccination.

The people of a republican state in Africa, as elsewhere, need a certain
civic awareness. And civic consciousness rises in groups that live not
only in cities but also within a district.

3   Administrative Legacy: II

One of the most important problems facing the newly independent
countries is the question of civil servants. The meager budgets of the
states are eaten up by personnel salaries. But that cost is not the only
problem. African republics have changed from white civil servants to
black ones, but they have not changed the structure of their administration.

With such an administration, unsuited to its needs, how can a poor
country achieve economic and social growth and assert full national
sovereignty on the national scene? This situation creates a politically
serious problem. The African civil servants do not blend harmoniously
into the masses because their standards of living and their life-styles are
so different from that of the population at large. This gap might create
tensions which could threaten the very independence of African countries.

Social and economic development implies, in Africa as elsewhere,
planning; this in turn requires, if not in all of the 80,000 villages of
French-speaking Africa, at least in the districts to which they belong, a
planner who knows local reactions, a coordinator who can arouse and
channel popular participation. Such a man cannot be a traditional chief,
an old bush administrator, or the foreign technician who stays only a
short time. He must be an African administrator helped by a team of
African civil servants of a new breed. Will he take the bush administrator's place?

To build a new type of government, and to recruit men able to take the
European administrator's place, this is what the African republics should
strive for. In these tasks lies the true test for newly independent
countries.

*The United Nations-administered World Health Organization (ed.).

4 On Decolonization

A False Analogy

We delude ourselves about decolonization in general, and particularly about decolonization in black Africa, when we compare it to American independence. We know that at the end of the eighteenth century England, and in the nineteenth century Spain and Portugal, lost their most important American colonies. These colonies obtained their independence through fighting and formed nations, one of which, the U.S.A., threw its heavy weight in favor of decolonization in Asia and Africa after the Second World War. But what we do not fully appreciate is the fact that Asian and African decolonization was of a very different nature and that it is false to attempt to draw a parallel with the American past. In America, independence showed the settlers' supremacy; in Asia and Africa, it meant their ouster.

Decolonization represents on the political level and, in a much more meaningful way, on the cultural level the rising of black and yellow peoples. They are not simply revolting against their former European mother countries, but against the concept of life itself as lived by the white man. They call the white man to account not only for what he did in their countries during the colonial period and the concepts he held of them, but also for what he does at home and his concept of himself—and they do so especially when he wants to cooperate with them. They do not accept the white man's assumption that his civilization possesses a universal superiority, that the colored peoples wanted decolonization only to adopt his civilization more completely. They reject that part of the white man which he thought was his brightest, most disinterested virtue, worthy of being spread to all men, his humanism, which for the black and yellow peoples is nothing but a facade for imperialism. They ask for complete decolonization, which implies the recognition and the development of their own civilizations. In this we have no common measure with American independence. In French-speaking Black Africa, for example, decolonization will mean the triumph of negritude, the affirmation in thought and action of Negro dignity and originality.

Decolonization in French-speaking Black Africa

A healthy cooperation implies a dialogue with negritude in French-speaking Black Africa. This dialogue may be profoundly jeopardized if we ignore the Franco-African conditions in which decolonization was achieved.

We should recall the colonial concepts which were adopted by the Third Republic. The Republic carried out colonization as a deed thought to be as glorious as free compulsory public education and universal suffrage, despite long-lived anticolonialism of different kinds among left- and right-wing public opinion.

Sixty years later, during the era of decolonization, the national duty is cooperation. Cooperation is a dialogue, and we will often emphasize this point later on. But in order to be able to cooperate, the country should face itself and show no sign of forgetfulness.

Black Africa, especially French-speaking Africa, will not develop if it isolates itself and distorts its past. Africa is becoming independent in the atomic age, when mankind has to choose between suicide and solidarity among the different nations. To opt for solidarity, to bring cooperation to human development, it must accept the entire past, colonization included. In Bertrand d'Astorg's novel, *La jeune fille et l'astronaute*, the heroine, a Parisian girl, tells the astronaut, an American: "A past which is still alive, that is civilization."

So too, in Africa, a young black girl might speak.

5   The Former Colonies and Their Historical Memories

Is there nothing in the colonial organization of public services that can be retained by Africa when it is planning its development? In the fields of education, sanitation, and rural organization is it a good idea to ignore the results obtained during the colonial era and to start from scratch in order to do better? Can it not be said that to consider Africa a tabula rasa is to reveal the worst form of colonialism? Cooperation means liberation from a negative anticolonialist attitude and listening to Africans who are aware of the responsibilities involved in the development of a country. Léopold Sédar Senghor wrote, in *Nation et voie africaine du socialisme*, in 1961: "When viewed in a historical perspective, the only fair one, colonization will appear as one of the forces of history. Races, peoples, nations, and more generally civilizations have always been in contact with one another, thus in conflict. Of course, conquerors bring ruin with them, but they also bring ideas and techniques which germinate and yield new crops."

6   Decolonization, the Mother Country, and History

What struck us French people about the independence movements that took place at an ever increasing speed from 1945 to 1962 was their

suddenness—a suddenness which blinded us instead of opening our eyes
to their common causes and their diverse shapes. We did not perceive
that they were not the same everywhere. They shot up like volcanic lava.
France was not alone, however, in being disoriented. All of Europe's
overseas empires were crumbling at about the same time, in the midst of
a political cataclysm whose uproar was noticed to the exclusion of its
profound significance. In fact a new order was in the making and was to
be a source of new problems.

Let us recall just a few dates in the history of the French empire: 1945,
the end of our mandate in Syria and Lebanon, and the beginning of the
Indochina war, which was to last until 1954; in 1954 Morocco became
independent; 1956, Tunisia gained its freedom while a special statute was
prepared for Black Africa and Madagascar, which became independent
in 1958–60; finally, in 1962, after a war which had been brooding since
1945 and broke out in 1954, we witnessed Algeria's independence. This
basic outline does not indicate the numerous changes in conditions
during which negotiations and fighting intermingled, sometimes to
initiate decolonization, sometimes to stop it. For seventeen years, the
average Frenchman, faced by a ruined homeland which urgently required
rebuilding, at the same time felt himself overseas the victim of the storms
that had led to independence. Decolonization was a process which
succeeding governments had been unable to detect in time or to control.
Many Frenchmen saw decolonization as a necessary evil rather than as
an opportunity to perform a new set of tasks: cooperation through
foreign aid.

Our collective memory remains obsessed by the Indochinese and
Algerian tragedies, which prevent us from realizing how different was
Black Africa's decolonization; in fact it looked like an amicable separation. Both parties agreed to separate, after fifty years of peace during
which there had been many dark moments but also some bright ones. To
appreciate this peaceful state we have only to count the few native
officers and outdated armaments found in the police force that sufficed
for the isolated administrators serving in the bush amidst African
populations who were far from being hostile to them and who often
showed congenial feelings which honored Africa and France.

The effect of decolonization on the former colonizers was to revive the
myth of the scapegoat. The mother country, out of her own sensitivity,
puts the burden of the colonial sin on the scapegoat and throws it out of
the city, thus purifying herself while believing that it is easier to decolonize
than to colonize. The best scapegoat is an innocent, a simpleminded
man. It is the civil servant or the settler or even the missionary who
believed in what he was doing overseas, who accomplished his task
without suspecting that colonization was evil and that he was a sinner.

How relieved is the mother country to be able to claim innocence now that the guilty one has been found! The one who had been asked to go to Africa is sent away to live in infamy. This naive man recalls in vain that his "justice-loving" mother country was not eager to provide him with the financial and technical means to establish and humanize an Empire— an empire in which she took great pride while not bothering to know its people or their needs. The matter is closed. Shame on the colonial administrator! He will watch, as an outcast. . . .

7   History and the Ex-Commandant

Bush administrators stopped sometimes in front of isolated tombs that would have remained unseen were it not for their piety which kept the spirit of the dead alive. The spirit of man still participates in the cosmos of life.

Because the bush administrator lived among and knew many diverse peoples, their mores, and their climates and because he experienced the identity of human nature, he was, in a way, a forebear of the cosmic age whose coming was prepared for by the erection of empires as well as by their destruction. He deserves to be remembered in death.

Aké Loba, an African writer, paid him the greatest tribute when he wrote in *Kocumbo, l'étudiant noir*: "To give oneself to someone who is not asking you to do so represents a remarkable feat, which, often, is neither understood nor appreciated." Such a gift was at the heart of the dual mission accomplished by the colonial administrator, who had, with meager means, to represent France to the Africans and to introduce and teach, as best he could, Africa to the French. What a pity if his dual mission ended by his being lonely in both communities, if he died misunderstood by a France and an Africa which can now say they never asked him to do anything. But the gift has been made and this alone matters. History—or legend—will pay tribute to him.

8   What Language for Africa?

In Black French Africa, French is the official language in schools. But does this solve the problem of deciding which language would be best for Africa?

No, say those who favor African languages. If schools want to be both African and modern, if they do not want to estrange their pupils from their familial milieu, then they should not start by using a language foreign to the pupils; nor should schools force them to think in a language which is not their own. Only an African language possesses the seeds capable of strengthening African minds. In the name of African identity and integrity, let us teach Africa and the modern world to African youth in an African language.

Those who favor French reply: very well, but which African language will be used? Which language will be chosen from among the 126 languages and dialects counted in AOF? Which African language will be given the political and social advantage of being the official language used in schools? And how will you prolong the use of it in books and newspapers outside school? A language used in teaching is not limited to the classroom. In order to live within school walls, it has to be used for all sorts of publications, especially for those which deal with the important research done on African life.

And those who favor French add: the existence of Black African poets, novelists, and writers in French letters proves that they lose nothing of their blackness in using and mastering the language of Marie Noël and Albert Camus. Léopold Sédar Senghor, a poet born in the small Senegalese town of Joal, puts down in French the stanzas of "Hosties noires"; Camara Laye, young Guinean author, writes in excellent French his novel entitled *Enfant noir*. How have they relinquished their own selves in order to don borrowed rags? Englishmen believe that our education Frenchifies Africans: "Africans learn to be French."* It would be more correct to say: French gives African multilingualism a very precious common language, a second native tongue through which it can freely express the continent's originality and freely draw from the treasure of a dual French and African culture. In the face of the problem caused by the language of instruction, I suggest the solution voiced by R. P. Charles: no language, no dialect can be rejected as being barbarian. All languages, all idioms can express nuances of feeling and intellectual reasoning. But for such a medium to be used, it has to meet three criteria. The language has to be actively spoken by enough people to allow worldwide exchanges. The country's elite has to actively make use of it. And finally it should be accepted by the population at large. I believe that French meets these three requirements in Western Africa.

9 The Future of the French Language and French Aid

French is used by the African Republics, not only on the international level among African states, to communicate among themselves but at home to promote economic and social development.

Internationally, French is the diplomatic language used by the fourteen republics from Mauritania to Congo-Brazzaville [former French colonies], to which we can add a fifteenth: Congo-Léopoldville, formerly

---

*The title of a famous study of French colonial education in Africa: William B. Mumford and G. St.J. Orde-Brown, *Africans Learn to Be French* (London, 1937) (ed.).

the Belgium Congo.* It is in French that they make themselves heard
during UN sessions, in committees and in specialized organizations, from
UNESCO to WHO and FAO. But however important the use of French is
in this arena, we will focus our attention on the inter-African scene.
There, French is the medium through which these countries can sign
agreements which we now will discuss.

Since their independence day, French-speaking republics have asserted
their desire to cooperate more closely by forming international organs
capable of serving their common interests, in the ideal of African unity.
They distrust any system which would legally place them in the position
of owing allegiance to France, as much as they desire to establish among
themselves organic relationships which will satisfy their innate need for
unity. So far, French has been the vehicle to gratify this innate need. It
had been the colonizers' tongue, and the colonized, in the most natural
fashion, adopted it as the most immediate and surest means of communicating among themselves and of forming the alliances or unions which
they felt were so necessary to them. The native tongues, however
important they might be for the elaboration of negritude, were not
adequate for insuring communication from state to state. Dialects, so
numerous even within each state (they number seventy, at least, in the
Ivory Coast), have not surged out of the precolonial past to perform the
role spontaneously and unanimously assigned to French by independent
Africa's political leaders.

Besides the OAU (Organization of African Unity), the French-speaking
countries have their own organization, which at first was UAM (African
and Madagascan Unity). The preliminary steps for its establishment were
taken during the Abidjan (October 1960) and Brazzaville (December
1960) conferences. The Yaounde (March 1961) and Tananarive (September 1961) conferences gave it its final shape. OAMCE (African and
Madagascar Organization for Economic Cooperation) was founded in
Brazzaville, in December 1960, in order to complement UAM, which was
then in the embryonic stage. The founders of UAM and OAMCE were
Mauritania, Senegal, Ivory Coast, Dahomey, Upper Volta, Niger, the
Cameroons, Gabon, Congo-Brazzaville, the Central African Republic,
Chad, and Madagascar. UAM stopped functioning in 1964, but in
February 1965, during the Nouakchott Conference, it was replaced by
OCAM (African and Madagascan Common Organization), while
OAMCE became UAMCE (African and Madagascan Union for Eco-
nomic Cooperation).

We thus have noted that independence was followed in the French-
speaking countries by a policy of unity and that this policy, in most
cases, was built through the French language. None of these countries

*Since the writing of this article it has become the Republic of Zaire (ed.).

withdrew into itself. And they too could express what M. Laurent Botokely, Madagascar's education minister, expressed at the yearly conference of national education ministers which took place in February 1964 at Tananarive: "French language and culture cement our national unity and allow us on the international level to understand one another; they back our friendship; they are one of the most important factors in our making progress toward African unity." Indeed, in each country, beyond the numerous tribes, national cohesion is acquired through a common language which is not one of the many African tongues but French.

Teaching French is, then, of primary importance. But M. Dannaud, director of cultural cooperation, calculates that only 10 percent of the population are real francophones in French-speaking Black Africa; only 4 million Africans understand French, and, among those, only 2 million speak and write it fluently.

What is disturbing is that this situation is worsening. Paradoxically, the tremendous progress achieved in education has led to a lowering of standards. Since schoolteachers—African as well as European—were overwhelmed by a flood of students, many classes had to be placed in the hands of untrained and inexperienced instructors. In Chad, the number of elementary students jumped from 55,000 in 1959 to 150,000 in 1964, but 90 percent of the classes are taught by partly trained instructors. In Niger, the percentage is 72 and in Gabon 70.

We should not forget that the men now in power have been trained in French schools. In a way, African independence has been nurtured by the French language; we could even say that it was conceived in French. Will the economic and social development be conceived in French, too? As of now, French seems to be linked to the progress achieved by the developing African nations. French does shine there, but it shines in a world limited by force of circumstance to only a few; this minority is the leaders, the elite, the few people responsible for the development without which French might only be a passing phenomenon. If we want French to grow deep roots in the masses and spread, it should be the language of social mobility and not only the tongue of a privileged class. M. Dannaud expresses this in the following manner: "If French attracts young Africans today, it is because it is directly linked to the hope for personal social promotion, for attaining a better life. If we had rendered 40 million Africans literate, the future of the French language would still be endangered if, at the time, Africa plunged deeper into poverty and chaos. A fundamental tie exists between the use of our tongue and a certain life-style." And Dannaud ends with the hope that the war against underdevelopment will continue successfully and that "the French language in twentieth-century Africa will become identified, as it did in eighteenth-century Europe, with the concept of progress and advance further as a result of the very development it will have given birth to."*

10   Duties and Difficulties of Foreign Aid

Decolonization means independence. But independence becomes meaningful only with social and economic development, and this in turn can be achieved only through cooperation with other countries. Black French-speaking Africa will not develop adequately if it counts only on its newly established states; the cooperation of richer and better equipped states is needed. Independence flourished with cooperation. This goes without saying but it is best to reflect upon it.

It seems easy enough to state the conditions for African development and to state that it can be achieved through cooperation. Three major and complementary tasks have to be handled: teaching, taking care of Africa's people, and feeding those people. These are the three challenges that confront cooperation in the framework of Africa's general development.

Can we just sit back and admire our manifestations of development— our three leading industries, automobile, steel, and tourism? It could easily be shown that we are unable to control the machines that enslave as much as serve us. Can we offer this as an example to developing countries? Will we applaud African development the day when cars kill as many people in the Cameroons as they do in Europe and the U.S.? Will we cheer the black student when, as proof of having become modern, she will say, as do her white sisters: "When I do not have my car, I feel lost!" Will we witness, with joy, signs of growth and progress such as urban concentration in Africa, traffic jams, overfilled buses, polluted air, and city people on edge because they spend two hours in the subway to and from an assembly-line job? And what about mass entertainment which, as we now realize, does nothing to regenerate either bodies or minds? A journalist, back from the Ivory Coast, told me that in Abidjan people stroll less than they used to and that they have quickened their pace. Will Abidjan soon be a city with rushed "lonely crowds"? Upon his return from Gabon, a missionary told me how, while walking on a road with a black child, the latter pricked up his ears when he heard the sound of an engine and even before seeing the truck pronounced the name of its make: Volvo. Is this black child on the right road to progress?

Conditions in Africa are forcing us to revise and even to question the

*Speech given to the Academy of Moral and Political Sciences, March 1965 [Delavignette's note].

ways in which we give technical assistance to the Third World. It is widely known that this aid is insufficient, badly distributed, and badly used. Facts speak for themselves: poor countries are getting poorer and poorer, and aid, as it is now understood, cannot help them. We are beginning to realize that aid is inefficient where it is a one-way interaction, that is, from donor to receiver, and that in order to become effective it has to result from a dialogue between the two parties about a mutual and genuine cooperation.

Negritude is conducive to such a dialogue, one in which all cooperating parties, African and others, respect one another and recognize that they are all human but at the same time diverse. Black awareness will prevent cooperation from leading to mere subsidized imitation and, through dialogue, will open up for Africa new ways to further its own development.

11   The Challenge to Young
Frenchmen in Africa

Cooperation requires its subjects to be committed. But the struggle is not easy! To impose on the young Frenchman in Africa, whether he be a Volunteer for Progress or an army volunteer,* the harsh life which "africanized" the bush administrator would be foolish. Can we say no to an air-conditioned and nicely landscaped villa; can we deprive ourselves of a refrigerator and electricity; can we set aside cars and walk again the paths during rounds of visits; should we wrap our legs to protect them against mosquitoes yet still catch malaria? In brief, can or should we do all this in order, it is hoped, to get a feel of Africa by living the way African masses do? No, cooperation does not expect that. It is meant to help Africa in its development, not to maintain its poverty. Of course, we would like the "cooperants" to have a sense of this poverty and to share some of its aspects.

Cooperation implies, if not a high degree of "commitment" leading to the sacrifice of oneself, at least reflection upon the difficulties which confront men of good will.

12   African Famine:
A Sign for Our Times

Faced by the famine which is devastating the Sahel, from Mauritania to Chad, through Senegal, Mali, Upper Volta, and Niger, how can we not

*Volunteer for Progress is the French equivalent of the Peace Corps. Instead of doing military service, young Frenchmen can serve as volunteers in development projects in Africa (ed.).

be impressed by the need to save the famished; there are millions of them! They live thousands of kilometers from us; but despite this enormous distance, their fate concerns us very closely.

Contrary to the false opinion which may still persist in France, Black Africa is poor in the hinterland and especially in the Sahel. There, under a harsh sky with irregular rainfall that can be skimpy or violently abundant, we find eroded soil, covered with unfertile laterite and very little humus, which bestows on the peasants a way of life wherein good years are a rarity.

We are not concerned here with folklore. If the fragile layer of humus is destroyed in the Sahel, if ponds and wells are dry, if the desert wins over man, then necessity will drive the rural family to the city, to the shantytown where it will disintegrate and its members become part of the proletariat. The internal balance of the African nations will be broken. The concentration of the urban population will increase in an unhealthy fashion while rural regions will die out.

Is such imbalance a problem only for African nations? No. The Sahel peasants and shepherds were shedding light on the values in our industrial civilization. Water, a vital element, is lacking in their lands; and we pollute rivers and oceans. The desert which is encroaching on Africans is a natural calamity against which an archaic civilization can do nothing. We in turn are spoiling nature, which is so favorable to us, by misusing it, and we unconsciously are making the preconditions of our own "desertification."

Let us help the Sahel countries and realize that the changes taking place in the relationships of man with nature, wherever they occur and for whatever reasons, concern all nations and contribute to or undermine the world balance.

13   A Dream

Under the aegis of the World Federation of Twin Cities, Banfora was declared a twin city of Chauvigny (Vienne department).

Far away from Banfora, but still in Upper Volta north of Ougadougou, the Sahel region is struck by a famine which decimates villages and herds. The old agrarian civilization based on shepherds and peasants is dying because of the "desertification" which is taking place. We must become aware that this tragedy which grips one part of mankind will ultimately rot the industrial civilization of the superpowers. May words and visits such as those exchanged between Banfora and Chauvigny lead world powers to act jointly with Africa in these dark moments.

We dream that the great superpowers of this world, instead of coupling their neoimperialism with empty humanitarian declarations, will establish a policy of genuine cooperation with countries that are handicapped by poor soil and climate, that lack the means to fight the desertification which slowly eliminates the subsaharan Sahel peasants. We dream. . . .

Sources

1. *L'Afrique noire française et son destin*, pp. 45–46.

2. "Des 'Commandants' français aux préfets africains," *Le Mois en Afrique* (February 1966), pp. 38–40.

3. *L'Afrique noire française et son destin*, pp. 148, 151–52, 155.

4. "Propos sur la décolonisation," *Académie royale des sciences d'outre-mer* [Brussels] (1967), pp. 208–9, 211, 214–15, 221.

5. *Du bon usage de la décolonisation* (Paris: Casterman, 1968), pp. 30–31.

6. Ibid., pp. 13–16, 25–26.

7. *L'Afrique noire française et son destin*, pp. 205–6.

8. "Les Problèmes de l'enseignement dans les territoires d'outre-mer," *Semaines sociales de France, 45e session, L'Enseignement, problème social* (Paris, 1958), pp. 348–49.

9. "Tiers monde sans tiers etat?" *Revue de Paris* 72 (December 1965): 84–86, 89–91.

10. *Du bon usage de la décolonisation*, pp. 33–34, 116–17.

11. Ibid., p. 58.

12. "Famine africaine: signe pour notre temps," *La Croix* (17–18 June, 1973), p. 18.

13. Memoirs, chap. 5, "A la base de l'Afrique des Paysans noirs," pp. 151–53, manuscript.

Bibliography

Albertini, Rudolf von. *Dekolonisation*. Cologne: Westdeutsche Verlag, 1966.

Alexandre, Pierre. "Le Problème des chefferies en Afrique noire française," *Notes et études documentaires*, 2508 (February 1959), 2–24.

Balandier, Georges. "Robert Delavignette, un libéral obstiné." *Le Monde*, February 10, 1976.

Betts, Raymond F. *Assimilation and Association in French Colonial Theory, 1890–1914*. New York: Columbia University Press, 1961.

Cohen, William B. *Rulers of Empire—The French Colonial Service in Africa*. Stanford, Calif.: Hoover Institute Press, 1971

Crowder, Michael. *West Africa under Colonial Rule*. Evanston, Ill.: Northwestern University Press, 1968.

Delavignette, Robert. "L'administrateur territorial en Afrique noire française." *Revue des Travaux de l'Académie des Sciences Morales et Politiques* 118 (1965): 83–96.

_____. *L'Afrique noire française et son destin*. Paris: Gallimard, 1962.

_____. *Afrique occidentale française*. Paris: Editions géographiques et maritimes, 1931.

_____. *Christianity and Colonialism*. Trans. by J. R. Foster. New York: Hawthorn, 1964.

_____. "Colo et chercheur," *Latitudes* (1963), pp. 5–9.

_____. "Connaissances des mentalités indigènes en A.O.F.," *Congrès international et intercolonial de la société indigène*, vol. 1 (Paris, 1931), pp. 553–66.

_____. "Décalages entre la colonisation et la connaissance," *Etudes Maghrébines—Mélanges Charles André Julien* (Paris, 1964), pp. 1–12.

_____. *Freedom and Authority in French West Africa*. London: Oxford University Press, 1950.

_____. "Pour les paysans noirs, pour l'esprit africain," *Esprit* 4 (1935): 367–90.

143

_____. "Tiers monde sans tiers état?" *Revue de Paris* 72 (December 1965): 82–91.

_____. "La vie de cercle au Soudan français," in André Siegfried, et al. *La Mer et l'empire* (Paris: Editions Jean-Renard, 1944), pp. 159–70.

Deschamps, Hubert. *Les méthodes et doctrines coloniales de France du XVIe siécle à nos jours.* Paris: A. Colin, 1953.

Girardet, Raoul. *L'idée coloniale en France.* Paris: La Table Ronde, 1972.

Lewis, Martin Deming. "One Thousand Million Frenchmen: The 'Assimilation' Theory in French Colonial Policy," *Comparative Studies in Society and History* 4 (January 1962): 129–53.

Mannoni, O. *Prospero and Caliban: The Psychology of Colonisation.* Trans. by Pamela Powesland. London: Methuen, 1956.

Morganthau, Ruth Schacter. *Political Parties in French-speaking West Africa.* New York: Oxford University Press, 1965.

Revue francaise d'histoire d'outre-mer, vol. 54 (1967). Issue devoted to Delavignette.

Suret-Canale, Jean. *Afrique noire, occidentale et centrale.* Vol. 2, *L'ère coloniale (1900–1945).* Paris: Editions sociales, 1964.

Weinstein, Brian. *Eboué.* New York: Oxford University Press, 1972.

Index

145

147

Index

Indigénat, 57
Indochina, 13–15, 39, 52, 79, 82, 92, 97, 109–19. *See also* Laos; Vietnam; Cochinchina
Ivory Coast, 5, 53, 54, 57, 64, 82, 84, 136, 138

Japan, 14, 109
Justice system, 89. *See also* Indigénat

Lamoricière, 122
Laos, 82
Laye, Camara, 135
League of Nations, 13, 21, 106
Lebanon, 133
Loba, Aké, 134
Local government, 58
Lugard, Lord, 80, 90

Macaulay, 32
Madagascar, 14, 39, 40, 79, 82, 85, 91, 92, 97, 98, 133, 136, 137
Mairey, Anne, 8
Mairey, Auguste, 3, 17
Mali, 92, 98, 139
Mandates, 83. *See also* Trusteeship
Martinique, 82
Maupoil, Bernard, 45
Mauriac, François, 15
Mauritania, 82, 91, 135, 136, 139
Mercier-Lacombe, 120–23
Ministry of Colonies, 1, 12, 14–15, 56, 83, 109
Ministry of Foreign Affairs, 82, 83
Ministry of Interior, 83
Mossis, 57
Morocco, 14, 15, 40, 73, 82, 133
Moutet, Marius, 10–11, 13, 47, 56–58

Nationalist movements, 14, 15, 79, 86, 94, 110–11, 111–19
Native policy, 51–52
Négritude, 2, 10, 131, 139
New Caledonia, 83, 97
New Zealand, 96
Niger, 4–6, 17, 31, 46, 82, 98, 136, 137, 139
Nigeria, 4–5, 68, 88
Niger River, 64, 65
Ninire, 104
Nkrumah, Kwame, 88
North Africa, 15–16, 39, 40, 41, 51,

83, 85, 99. *See also* Algeria; Morocco; Tunisia
Nouakchott Conference, 136

Oran, 120
Ouattara, 5
Oubangui, 82
Ouezzin Coulibaly, 12
Ougadougou, 5, 32, 140
Ousman Dan Fodio, 54
Outrey, Max, 38

Pakistan, 95
Pavie, Auguste, 45
Paysans noirs, 7–9, 12, 20, 35, 36
Popular Front, 1, 10, 47, 56–58
Portugal, 77, 93, 95, 131
Présence africaine, 2
Press, 50, 73–74, 120
Protectorates, 83

Rabelais, 52
Racism, 59–60, 61, 81, 101, 103, 106. *See also* Africans, French image of
Regional cooperation, 60–61, 135–38
Representation, political, 82–85, 89, 91–93, 96–98, 102–5, 106–7
Residency, 28–31
Réunion, 82, 83, 90, 91, 97
Rome, 77, 97
Roume, Ernest, 38
Roupnel, Gaston, 3, 17
Rufisque, 76

Saint-Louis, 50, 76
Saint Pierre and Miquelon, 83
Salan, General, 120
Samory, 53, 54
Sansanding dam, 57
Schoelcher, Victor, 77
Sections administratives spécialisées, 124
Senegal, 50, 54, 55, 64, 75–77, 82, 83, 84, 91, 92, 98, 136, 139
Senghor, Léopold, 2, 11, 12, 17, 80, 87–88, 132, 134
Service africain, 12
Settlers: in Algeria, 83; in Cameroons, 81, 106
Sierra-Leone, 88
Slavery, 22, 54, 59, 64, 77, 90
Somaliland, 18, 83